D1246480

Atlantis Books

www.atlantisbooks.org

AEGEAN NOTEBOOKS

Other books by the author in English

The Lost Center and Other Essays in Greek Poetry
The Drama of Quality: Selected Essays

ZISSIMOS LORENZATOS

AEGEAN NOTEBOOKS

REFLECTIONS
BY SEA AND LAND
IN THE
ARCHIPELAGO

Translated by
LIADAIN SHERRARD

DENISE HARVEY (PUBLISHER) · LIMNI, EVIA, GREECE

First published in 2013 by Denise Harvey (Publisher)
340 05 Limni, Evia, Geece
www.deniseharveypublisher.gr

This book was originally published in Greek
by Domos Books, Athens, in 1983, with the title
Στοῦ Τιμονιοῦ τὸ Αὐλάκι [*In the Wake of the Rudder*]

Cover photograph by Vassilis Gerontakos

Printed and bound in Greece by Alphabet S.A.

ISBN 978-960-7120-31-1

Aegean Notebooks
is the nineteenth publication in
THE ROMIOSYNI SERIES

. . . for the place whereon thou standest is holy ground.

(Exodus 3 : 5)

CONTENTS

TRANSLATOR'S NOTE

In one of his Notebooks, Zissimos Lorenzatos says: 'The present text does not require footnotes'. I have taken this as a statement of intent: even though he eventually published these journals, he is careful to emphasize that they were written under sail, and that they are above all the expression of a present that was being lived moment by moment, not recollected in tranquillity at a later date (apart from some subsequent insertions which he specifically identifies). In order to be read as such, it has been decided to minimize the footnotes as far as possible, limiting these to the couple he provides himself plus a few definitions of the Greek words which appear. Nevertheless, as many of the Greek themes that are touched upon may be largely unfamiliar to the foreign reader, these have been marked by an asterisk which indicates an endnote where the reader will find them explained.

In addition, there are half a dozen phrases in the Greek text which I have omitted to translate altogether. These are chiefly where the writer uses dialect words to make a point, or where he throws in an allusion that is instantly understandable to a Greek person but which would require a lengthy and laborious explanation for a non-Greek, and would — in my judgement — obstruct the flow for the reader. I should stress that in none of these cases has the meaning of the text been compromised.

Translations of the French quotations will also be found following the endnotes.

Any passages of poetry quoted in the text with no attribution are by the author and translated by myself.

It seemed appropriate to include a translation (also by myself) of the lovely poem 'Sea Timbers' ('Θαλάσσια Ξύλα') by Lorenzatos at the end of the Notebooks, primarily because in it he reiterates in a different form the main preoccupations and themes of the text. 'Sea Timbers' was not published in his lifetime, but was found among his papers after his death and published as a private monograph on the 3rd of February 2005.

Special thanks are due to the author's daughter, Pierretta Lorenzatou, for her meticulous contribution to the final text.

PROLOGUE

The story of the wanderings which were ultimately written up in the *Aegean Notebooks* had its beginning towards the end of May 1975, on the upper floor of a café in Kolonaki Square, Athens. This is how it came about:

At that time, having heard about Zissimos from a mutual friend, but without ever having met him, I sent him a recent book of mine. In reply I received a charming and somewhat curious letter, which ended with the phrase: 'more on this, if we happen to meet one day!' I telephoned him at once and we met, having arranged how we were to recognize each other, at the café mentioned above.

At that first meeting, which lasted over two hours, and after he had asked me some details about my book, the conversation turned by chance to the subject of the sea, and there it remained. I had been crazy about the sea from childhood and for years had had a little motor-boat which I went around in, but I had now just bought a small sailing boat of English make. Like me, Zissimos was irresistibly drawn to the Grecian sea. Although he had no previous sailing experience, during the preceding summer of 1974 he had accompanied a close childhood friend of his, who later became a friend of mine as well, Venetis Kougeas — later rector of the Higher School of Agronomy — on a trip around Cape Maléas, in a small wooden boat a mere 5.50 metres in length! This trip is described in the first notebook, while the rest of the book is about the trips we made together in my sailing boat.

Thus, after the two-hour conversation in the café, when the time came for us to part, I said to him: 'Zissimos [a short while previously, at his request, we had left off using the polite form to each other], perhaps the time has come for you to do something utterly crazy with your life. You've only just met me. In two weeks or so, I'm going off with my girlfriend for a month or more to the Aegean, without any fixed itinerary, just drifting around. Trust your instinct, decide to do it and come along with me for as long as you like.' He looked at me without speaking for a little and then replied simply: 'I'll come.' And he did.

That was the beginning, and the rest is what you'll read in the book…

The 'Captain'
George Pamboukis

AUTHOR'S FOREWORD

When I set out to write about some recent summers that I spent sailing in Greek waters, and began to put in order certain thoughts that occurred to me in relation to this country, I reflected that if you don't look on writing as an art similar to the ancient arts which preceded it, such as the art of painting, or the potter's wheel, or the jeweller's craft, which arrive at a result which is of some ultimate use to us in our lives, then nothing remains but a falsehood, or else a vain attempt to talk about life, not in its own words — for life doesn't speak — but in yours, and by writing about it to somehow live it over again, apart from the one and only time that you actually can and do live it; for life itself writes nothing, it erases everything that is written about it, and simply, irreplaceably *lives*, like the inaccessible 'well of water springing up' in St John's Gospel. Thus, the observations which follow are not intended to portray anything. Life is what we live, it is a fruit that we eat, and when you write about it you are, at most, chewing over its peel. Life is not work, whereas writing is. All work includes materials and labour — you reckon on so much for one and so much for the other, and thereby get an idea of what the work is worth. The art of writing uses language as its material. It has become difficult these days not to adulterate one's materials, and it is even more difficult not to inflate the charge for the labour. I look on writing as an art which I struggle to get right in so far as I am able, so that it can be somehow useful to us in our life — as the goldsmith's piece of jewellery is useful, or a pot, or a painting — without troubling myself any further as to whether this usefulness will gain a more universal acceptance, or whether the written works will be regarded as 'works not demonstrably useful', as Papadiamándis* put it.

The few observations collected in this volume owe their existence to the fact that I was lucky enough to be invited to accompany some good friends of mine on their trips, and used the opportunity to experience and record what follows in the form in which it was dictated to me, either by my tiny notebooks or by the circumstances. Certain enlargements, or digressions, that I make on some of the themes came later, since they required a more detached treatment. There are thus some anachronisms in the text (in a notebook from 1974 I may refer to a book published in 1980, or to a recent event in an entry which predates it). This changes nothing; for as Aristotle says in his *Poetics*, 'poetry is more philosophical and a higher thing than history'.

Even though, to all appearances, they do not resemble my other writings — which are essays for the most part — I publish these observations today in case they prove to be of use in a more general sense (unlike a purely personal experience), more relevant and more unmistakably linked to this beloved island-strewn land of our fathers.

I take the years in turn from the beginning, starting the entries with each day's journey; all the digressions were first written when we were out at sea, with the wake of the boat unfurling behind us.

THE NOTEBOOKS

FIRST NOTEBOOK 1974

15th–20th July, Cephalonia. At this time of year the high point is the swimming, and the clarity and purity of the sea (for how long, I wonder?). On the last day of the return journey there was the call-up (20th) and I took the boat to Glaréntza. Appalling conditions on board. At dawn of the next day the Turks landed on Cyprus. Thus we have come full circle since the process was initiated for Greece by Papágos and his followers in 1954* (I'm not talking about the British and the Turks, they've got their own agenda). We're now in the year 1974. For 20 years, if I'm not mistaken, we've gone looking for trouble and we've reaped what we sowed. *Gâvurun akili sonradan gelir,* as the Turks say, meaning: the Greek's wisdom comes after the event. I would add that it doesn't even come after, it comes rarely or not at all.

15th August. On the evening of the Feast of the Virgin we took the *Kálymnos* to Neápolis (Vátika).

> *Down at Vátika*
> *Down at Velanídia*
> *I found my true love*
> *And she was planting onions.*

16th. 'When you sail round Cape Maléas, forget your home', said Strabo. The next day, we crossed the mountain by car and went down to Velanída. End of the world. White houses on the mountain slope, facing due east with the north-east wind blowing straight down on them. We made our way to the sea on foot — you can't get down to the bay by car — launched the boat and set out about 10 o'clock in the morning in windy weather. (The previous evening we had bought anti-fouling paint at Vátika for the boat, but when we saw the weather we decided to leave it for later or when another occasion presented itself.) We raised the sail, passed out beyond the little dusky islands and the sub-merged rocks which are everywhere (terrifying in bad weather) and doubled Cape Maléas with a light northeast wind behind us. Away in the distance we could see Tsirígo [Kíthyra] and could just make out a caique with a sail, like the description in a rather inferior verse of Victor Hugo's poem 'Cérigo':

Au loin court quelque voile hellène ou candiote

Our boat flew along, past the lighthouse which clings to the huge rock, reminding those who have been there of the Chozoviótissa monastery on Amorgós. From above the light-housemen waved to us and we waved back at them from below. We breasted some heavy swells, still flying along, and reached the two little chapels, dedicated I think to St George and St Irene (you can get there along a goat-track). The diffi-cult part was over. The dragon had been slain by St George and Irene (peace) followed after. This is what the chapels seem to be telling us.

It may be remembered that the cape did not always prove so easy, as in the case, for instance, of the dishevelled Maniote woman who lost both her husband and her father at once, and extemporised the following lament over them:

Tsirígo and Kavomaliá
The sea is covered with sails
One hour, one moment, was enough
To make me a widow and fatherless.

We sailed all day and in the evening we anchored at Eliá, the tiny port of Mólai.

17th, Saturday. At 3.50 a.m. we headed for Gýtheion — known as Marathoníssi in 1821 — straight across the Gulf of Laconia, a distance of eleven miles. The wind was gusting off-shore. Behind us, in the east, the dawn sky was black. Dimly chalked in the depth of the sky were one or two lingering stars, which you guessed at rather than saw. 'Diamants extrêmes...', as Paul Valéry cryptically calls them in his poem 'La Jeune Parque'. The crossing took us two hours. We were headed for the Mani, which is almost home for me because of the K's (old family friends and bound to us by the ties of *koumbariá*,[1] ever since my mother, God rest her, baptized my friend's twin brother, who died young). Going there always makes me feel glad and full of energy. I love the hard earth and the stony heat of the place, the Maniote sun.

We left Gýtheion and headed south. In the wake of the boat float ribbons of seaweed, phanerogamous plants, escapes from the Saronic Gulf, where you never see them nowadays. Seaweed too has become scarcer almost everywhere along the coasts.

The little boat had come to Velanídia all the way from

[1] *Koumbariá* is the relationship, of great significance in Greece, between a couple and their best man/woman, or between the god-parents of a child and the child's parents (the first case usually but not always leads to the second), and it extends to the whole family on both sides.

Salamis. My friend had sailed her there by himself, accompanied by his pointer bitch Lara, and now we were going on together to Kitriés, the harbour at Dolí, where the boat was to be left permanently. (My friend left from Koúlouri [Salamis] the day I was leaving for Cephalonia, which was why we couldn't travel together. Before Kavomaliá [Cape Maléas] he was stopped by bad weather, a strong westerly gale, and by the call-up, and he tacked to Velanídia, where he found two fishermen to take care of his boat.)

The boat is strongly constructed, with mulberry wood planking, which lasts for ever, and ribs and sternpost of pine, built by the boatbuilder Psarós at Pérama, 5.55 metres long and 1.85 wide, too small for such long runs, with a four-and-a-half horsepower Petter engine, like the ones which Lloyds has approved for lifeboats. In the bows of the boat were two anchors of four flukes, with another small one in the forecastle for catching on rocks or stones on the shore, and in the stern was a folding sand anchor with two flukes, what they call a *pinélo*. We had a British Admiralty map, the section showing Venetico to Spezzia, and a compass.

In starting to talk about the boat and to call things by their names in the language which comes naturally to us (*'naturalis'*, as Dante says), I thought about the Sisyphean struggle of those who buried the natural names, generated and sanctified by the invincible breath of life itself, under spadefuls of the soil of an unnatural or artificial (*'artificialis'*) formula, so that now you have to unearth every living word — if you can find it recorded anywhere — from beneath these heaps of soil, whenever you need to have recourse to the relevant dictionaries or encyclopaedias.* So much labour lost, so much time wasted, in order to dress life up; and to what end? Was it to fill up the immense space ('l'espace immense') which Koraïs saw as separating us from the goal that he worshipped and longed for? It was then the 16th January 1803, 'le 16 Nivôse'. Fill it up: was it likely? Just as the month of Nivôse was born dead, so was our attempt at ancestral revival. 'La nation contemple pour la première fois le spectacle hideux de son ignorance, et frémit en portant ses regards sur l'espace immense qui la sépare de la gloire de ses ancêtres.'(Coray, *Mémoire sur l'état actuel de la civilization dans la Grèce*, Paris 1903.) It all sounded very credible. Today, we know what it amounted to and we are still trying to cover up our humiliation. Those who dreamed of ancestral glory failed to realize that the glory of modern Greece — every nation has its own glory — was crowned neither with the olive of the ancients nor with the diadem of Byzantium, but with the simple wreath of glory described by Solomós:*

> *And her head is adorned with a circlet*
> *Fashioned out of the sparse-growing grasses*
> *That were left on the desolate earth.*

This might not be the wonderful wreath of antiquity or the brilliant one of the Byzantines, but it is our own. Had they understood this, we would not have spent so many years paying the penalty. You open an encyclopaedia and look up the entry for a horse's harness and find a complete perversion of the common terms for bridle, reins, bit etc. It is like burying the living in order to raise up the dead. I could understand it if the words didn't exist; but even then you have to respect the phonetics, the forms and the syntax of a language before you lay hands on it. To set aside existing words and replace them with your own, like an orthopaedic surgeon — such an abomination has never been attempted in any other country. Whole teams of people laboured for years at this systematic earthing over, setting aside thousands of living names (chief among these teams were the universities, the polytechnics, the military academies and all scholarly institutions in general, the mints of Greek learning, what Koraïs called in his writings 'les collèges') and now you have to seek under the earth, doing the same work in reverse, to find an arm here, or a leg there, which are still visible and which beckon strangely to you, with a living smile, from amidst the general deadness. We are now obliged to begin the process of exhuming all this treasure which has been swept aside, what used to be our common speech and fortunately has never ceased to be spoken by ordinary people. But something else took place as a result of this aggressive act of changing the language. We learned words artificially that were never in use prior to a few hundred years ago, and that replaced the older, natural ones, which were thus stopped in their tracks and artificially unlearned. In this manner the language is squeezed dry, its juice is extracted and it becomes antiseptic and sterile. Most importantly, we deliberately close off the water in the furrow, we cut off the current of language which runs outwards in the service of wisdom and which Plato in the *Timaeus* considered to be the most beautiful and the best of all currents: 'but the river of speech, which flows out of a man and ministers to the intelligence, is the fairest and noblest of all streams'. I fear that we do not get to understand our forbears through speech, but by means of intelligence! If we had intelligence we would learn also that the river of language is not only the fairest and noblest of all streams, it is a wine made holy by the inviolable spiritual power of all speech, which, as Roman Jakobson points out in relation to the mystery of the Divine Eucharist, constitutes 'the greatest privilege that was ever granted to people, for the words pronounced by the priest are the invocation of a miracle even greater than God's creation of the world' (R. Jakobson and K. Pomorska, *Dialogues,*

Paris 1980). This is assuming, of course, that we are believers, whether like Solomós when he takes his oath:

By the immaculate mysteries on which I trembling swear

or like T. S. Eliot when he addresses all his readers in general using similar language (the word 'tremendous' at the end echoes Solomós's 'trembling'): 'I doubt whether what I am saying can convey very much to anyone for whom the doctrine of Original Sin is not a very real and tremendous thing' (*After Strange Gods,* 1934).

Needless to say, what happened to our language happened to us, and the question is, what are we doing now? Initially, what was needed was for us to find names for a whole number of things that were gradually flooding into our lives from every direction or which we were using for the first time — things not just in the world outside us but also in the inner world (concepts) — but this undertaking should have followed its normal course, using the phonetics, forms and grammar of the natural language, instead of despising it and attempting to sweep aside, by a kind of *coup d'état*, thousands of names which were already in existence. Enriching a language with more words, even if these are formed naturally — enriching it with more vocabulary, quantitatively — is not enrichment. It has been calculated that in Shakespeare's time the English language contained about 150,000 words. Now it has 600,000 — but no Shakespeare. With the aid of foreign manuals and instruction books, rules and lists of proper names, the teams I referred to above engaged in translations far removed from the phonetic, formal or grammatical basis of the language today, and in consequence they upset, distorted and seriously delayed that natural development of a linguistic sense which would have taken place had it not been for this attempt at orthopaedic surgery. Now, we need to labour at doing the same thing in reverse, and it makes one marvel at how casually some people determine the general course to be followed by an entire nation, even with regard to the language. Now, even our revisions will be dogged by all the errors that resulted from the ill-fated ancestral revival, and from the signs it is already clear that there will be no lack of people — of the opposite persuasion this time — who will determine, equally casually, on various miracle cures with which to treat an entire nation. We are paying the penalty. But the way ahead now looks better than it did, and the general tone strikes a brighter note amidst the surrounding darkness.

There was one other thing that Koraïs failed to observe. In order to create a literature and to continue to create one, in order to forge a culture, we need to have in our possession a language that is constantly changing. Language is like water: running water you can trust, but you should never drink water that has been standing. Language remains alive and flowing when it is constantly changing. You can bend down to it and drink fearlessly of the water of life. A dead, stagnant language never changes. Anyone who tries to create literature out of a static, unchanging language has no choices, and the most they can do is of necessity to imitate the original examples of writing in the language, with no possibility that they will ever match them, since the latter were created out of a natural language and not an artificially manufactured one. Civilization does not come out of a laboratory but out of life, where it either ascends Kálvos's* 'difficult cliffs' or, without life to sustain it, sinks away.

After Gýtheion we made Skoútari — the swimming is good there — and then Kótronas, which is in the next bay along. The north-east wind whipped up the waves and we got wet (from squalls, as when we were going up the Laconian gulf from Vátika to Eliá).

18th, Sunday. We set sail from Kótronas about an hour before dawn. We passed Pórto Káyio, Vathí Livádi and Stérnes — a few years previously we had walked over all that area, one summer when we stayed at the lighthouse with the lighthouse-keepers — and we doubled Cape Taínaron at 8.30, with the wind still blowing from the north-east, and the sea behind us unreeling the endless yarn of itself ever more swiftly and liberally.

> *Stay forty miles*
> *Off Cape Matapán*
> *And twice forty more again*
> *Off Cape Grósso.*

The verse refers to the pirates, but it could equally well be a reference to the weather. Two interpretations, one piratical, one maritime.

Thus we reached the shadowed region of the Mani, and started to go up the Messenian Gulf. In our haste we missed the cave of Hades, which we had come alongside last time, a few years ago, when we were staying with the lighthouse-keepers. There is, I remember, a foreign melody by Jean-Philippe Rameau, with the words 'Profonds abîmes du Ténare...'

As I was saying, we had stayed, again the two of us, in the lighthouse with the lighthouse-keepers. I remember that it was the month of July, 1970 — I am digressing here for a moment — and we reached Taínaron on the eve of the 26th, the feast of St Paraskeví. The sea below the rocks was the roughest and deepest water I have ever swum in. They told us that in winter, during the great storms, the waves sometimes rear up as high as the lighthouse, so they must be several metres high. We went for a trip by caique to Solotéri one day; another time we walked all day, past

Stérnes with its ancient mosaic, now grass-grown and crumbling (a solar symbol, I should think, in the form of a circle), past Kokkinóyia Mianés, on to Marmári and as far as Pórto Káyio.

On that occasion we stayed about ten days at the lighthouse, and shared with the two lighthouse-keepers and their wild dog, Arápis, a life cut off from the world, austere, monotonous and sodden with moisture. The few lighthouses left which are still manned hold the attraction that Cameroon or the Persian Gulf hold out nowadays, as places where Greeks go (we were always a nation which exported our poverty), saying: I'll go and spend X number of years there and make X amount of money for my home and children. This was in some sense the way in which the lighthouse-keepers regarded their voluntary imprisonment, consoled by the prospect of an earlier retirement than is normal in other branches of employment. Other prospects, apart from the settled salary and the prompt pension, are few: mostly a bit of rheumatism or some related ailment. Food was a problem: fish was occasionally to be had, weather and luck permitting. Every morning at dawn, for no apparent reason, Arápis barked fit to wake the dead. No one could make him shut up. Until one morning, almost before light, going towards Stérnes, we saw a jackal running up the stony slope to vanish over the pass.

At the end of the day, something always remains of one's childhood dreams. When I was a child I thought of becoming a lighthouse-keeper. I am now cured of that particular sickness, but am still caught up in the solitude syndrome. In the solitude of a lifetime I have learned, gradually, to do the work I do.

End of digression.

To our left, out at sea, was Karavópetra, a rock like a submerged tree with its tufted top sticking up from the water. In midsea an antlion flew swiftly past us, heading for the land. What on earth was the creature doing so far out?

We swam in a bay and at midday anchored at Yeroliména for lunch. At two in the afternoon we continued up the gulf and for one whole hour, no less — five miles — we passed close to and under Cape Grósso. This is no child's play but a terrifying experience, and in a small boat the cape seems to go on for ever. There were no waves, but the waters boiled around us, having nowhere to go along all its length. The pitching of the boat was like being in a milk churn, or like when we thump the bottom of the boat in order to frighten the fish into going into the nets. It's a rock like one of the monsters out of the Apocalypse, awe-inspiring. 'I shall remember it for the rest of my life', said my friend to me the other day. The cliffs are upwards of two hundred metres high, eaten away by the sea, and the water at their feet is dark and turbulent. What student of the impossible — what craftsman or wise lover of beauty — raised upon this monstrous rock the Castle of Oriá?

> *And twice forty more again*
> *Off Cape Grósso.*

We made certain beyond doubt of the maritime meaning of the verse. The other, piratical, meaning has been overtaken for the moment by history. We shall see what happens later.

Plants that grow on the rocks: prickly pear, capers, thornbushes or parasitic plants whose names I don't know. Birds: falcon, wild dove, kingfisher. Before coming to the end of this fearful monster of chthonic power and arrogance, there is a little church, dedicated to the Virgin of Mercy, fifty metres or more up the crag and about a hundred metres below the top, in an inaccessible cleft, built perhaps in fulfilment of a vow, perhaps as a hermitage, or something else: a token of faith, a cry from the heart. The rock exuded heat (it was August) and seared us with its burning breath. Its enormous height and surface area stored radiant heat like a furnace. As soon as we had passed it the world regained its freshness, the wind blew softly. We were free of the churning sea and the violent rocking of the boat, as though someone had taken us on horseback across a cool river.

We anchored at Dirós, where we slept that night outside a tavern belonging to one of the locals, beneath an awning of straw, some distance away from the famous caves, the sound and light spectacle and the various tourist attractions.

19th. We continued our journey, fishing as we went. Liméni is beautiful, with the crumbling Mavromichális* castle left to its fate of decay, as is the case in many places in Greece. (It was later 'restored' by some descendant of the family now resident in Switzerland. This is all to the good; the trouble is that it is now starting to crumble all over again.) We collected fine salt off the rocks round Trachíla for our lunch of fish soup. We made Selínitsa and then on to Kalogriá (Stoúpa) for a swim and the midday meal. Untrodden sand, clear transparent water. In the sea were two or three springs or whirlpools, from which fresh water wells up. The circular eyes of the water were like liquid threshing floors. Early in the afternoon we anchored off Kitriés, the harbour of Dolí and the last stage of our journey. The little boat had reached its destination; from now on it would remain here.

For the remaining days, which amounted to a week, we fished, swam, and walked, living mainly up at Dolí, where my friend had various things to do and certain repairs to put in hand in his family house, and we used Kitriés as our country resort and a place to commune with the sea. To go up from Kitriés to Dolí took about an hour or more, through olive groves, scattered stone terracing, patches of vegetables and plots of land planted with fruit trees. On leaving we saw the first cyclamen, and we were accompanied by a downpour, the first rains of autumn, with thick impenetrable mist and huge lightning flashes. A lot of water fell that day.

Since we were speaking earlier about language and the reprehensible 'immense space' ('l'espace immense') which separates us, apparently to our detriment, from our glorious ancestors, I will continue along the same lines and say a few words about Greek learning and classical literature — *literae humaniores*, as Greek and Latin were known in Europe four hundred years ago, as opposed to sacred learning. This was the first and correct meaning of so-called *humanismus*, humanism, which today has lost all meaning, since we are at liberty to assign to it any meaning we want.

First of all, there is the general pretence that contemporary society, in England or Germany, say, represents the classical values of the ancient Greek world and can claim descent from them — a world that considered and defined technology as vulgar, that was based (as always in antiquity) on the institution of slavery, and whose cities and mentality prove that freedom in 5th century BC Athens and freedom in 19th century London are about as alike as an Attic vase and the Industrial Revolution. This striking dissimilarity, which only someone who is pretending, or who has misunderstood the monuments to an unlikely degree, can claim to ignore, inevitably meant that the study of the ancient world became at best a theoretical preoccupation, resulting in a few great works of synthesis and innumerable smaller works concerned with analysis, in which the texts were published, commentated, footnoted, and reconstructed with ever-increasing accuracy, until the preoccupation with them was confined to one area, the literary laboratories, separated from reality or from people's lives — something which had never happened before to these texts, of course (if we except the literary laboratories of Alexandria). Later scholars praised the classical virtues, and later societies constituted the living antitheses of those virtues. Europe tried to pretend that 'le miracle grec' was the main spiritual tradition underlying its civilization, a civilization utterly and completely at odds with what is fragmentarily communicated by all the monuments which have had the equivocal fortune to come down to us, whether entire or mutilated. Yet the antique prototype bore, and could bear, no relation (and I am not sure that it should) to its hypothetical descendant, western civilization. Archytas's pulley and Edison's light bulb belong not just to different civilizations but to different worlds. Later technology concentrated on the monuments and confined itself to a technical investigation of them (to a degree approaching perfection). In some of these cases, the physical sciences proved astonishingly useful. Radiometric dating undertook to accurately solve problems of chronology which went back 45,000 years. (The margin was enough and to spare, archaeologically and historically speaking, if we consider that Neanderthal *Homo primogenitus* goes back 50,000 years.) Spiritual searching was everywhere pushed aside by conventional research. Our attitude to Plato became the same as the attitude adopted by the physical sciences towards cell growth or the stellar orbits. Thus, attention was fatally transferred from the spirit which 'giveth life' to the letter that 'killeth'. The conventional learning of Greek — or Latin — became an end in itself, and whoever had a conventional knowledge of the language was considered to have a knowledge of the classical spirit and the capacity to interpret it or teach it to others. But what value can be attached to a formal study for which there is no use in real life? The ancient texts are not to be read theoretically but proven in practice, since the purpose of writing them was always the 'best life' (as Aristotle says in his *Politics*), not some theoretical aspiration, and only by living them — directly and practically, not indirectly and theoretically — will they come to be understood by the person who makes them his study. Merely knowing the language is not enough. In the case of Plato, for instance, one could justifiably, *mutatis mutandis*, adopt the following comparison: 'It is evident,' writes Ananda Coomaraswamy, 'that in order to understand the Vedas, a knowledge, however profound, of Sanscrit is not enough. (The Indians themselves on this issue do not base themselves on their understanding of Sanscrit, but insist on the absolute necessity of study with a guru.)' (*A New Approach to the Vedas*, London, 1933.) From this point of view, a knowledge of Greek eventually came to be a concealment of ignorance. (I am not saying that the spirit of the ancients can be approached without some knowledge of the language, I am saying that it definitely cannot be attained through this knowledge alone.)

One of the results of this contradiction, in our country, was the open conflict in the matter of the language, resulting in the rigidity and inflexibility with which we are all familiar. This linguistic civil war, which was the natural offspring of Greek learning and the *literae humaniores* in their ill-fated opposition to reality or human life, could be said to have literally destroyed us in every respect over the last hundred years. I say 'in every respect' because the civil war of language has penetrated every corner of society — and of politics as well, it hardly needs saying — and its offshoots have encouraged that deplorable Greek dissension which Solomós anathematized from the very beginning. 'And what can I say about the present? Corruption is so widespread and so deeply-rooted that it bewilders one', he wrote in a (translated) letter to Tercetti, possibly in 1842, the

Italian original of which has yet to be discovered and published. One of the decisive elements in the 'widespread corruption' since then is undoubtedly the language question.

If someone were to sit down now and discuss the details
and go over the particulars of our country's linguistic divisions,
I don't believe it would alter anything about this unhappy
situation. What we fail to take into account is that language
determines thought, and the quality of the language determines the quality of our thinking, since the latter is subject to
the former and not *vice versa*. No one can know either of them
ab extra. You may shed your skin, but you can never shed your
language. You live inside it. You can't build a bridge out into
space and get to know your language and your thought from
there. In his relationship with his language, man can unite
with it in repeating St Paul's teaching '...then shall I know
even as also I am known', and stop at that point. He can go no
further. For man, the limit of language — in the widest sense
of the term — is identical with the limit of knowledge — all
or any language and all or any knowledge, from music to
mathematics. In order to live and develop within that limit
you need to be absolutely honest in your language and your
thinking, and to engage in a hard daily struggle with the all-
powerful law of inertia, since you will be fighting against the
current while everyone else will be going with the flow. To the
degree that we divide up our language, we divide or mutilate
our thinking. When you study the cultural monuments of the
language and the various linguistic mechanisms, the same
thing can happen to you as happens with life, if you allow
yourself to be totally distracted or carried away by the things
that happen to you, in joy and in sadness, important or sec-
ondary, and thus lose sight of life itself.

In conclusion, as regards this whole sad business one cannot forgive those who, whether in the Universities or the other

schools, equipped with a purely formal knowledge of the language with all its accoutrements (linguistics, syntax, grammar, technique), made us look on the ancient writers as hateful or inaccessible. The few exceptions owed their exceptionality, essentially, not so much to a more correct teaching method or theory, but because they were a particular kind of individual. Such individuals enhance the work that they do or the art that they know. The person behind every work and every art is important. In the final analysis, men, as Makriyánnis* said, make enlightenment, and not *vice versa*. And in this respect the illiterate general knew more, it would seem, than all the learned men of letters.

SECOND NOTEBOOK 1975

12th June. Set sail at 8.30 a.m. At 7.30 p.m. arrived at Sérifos, Cape Kýklopas. 8.15 p.m. Cape Spathí, ditto.

13th, Friday. 9.30 a.m. set out for Kímolos from Livádi. This time the boat is 5 tons, around 9.50 metres in length. Motor sailing.

14th. Depart from the little harbour of Psátha, on Kímolos (we had gone up to the village) at 9.15 a.m., with the island of Pólyvos (ancient Polýaigos) on our left, making for Folégandros:

> *Dead calm. Soon there are scales on the sea's skin*
> *Then lakes, as when you stoop to look into a* pithári,[1] *then*
> *more scales*
> *To the south the sea is one seamless expanse: all morning,*
> *all the time, as far as eye can see.*

Someone attempted to spell out the rhythm of our journey, to convert it through words back into its original components, like a cock which flaps its wings for a moment as if to fly and then starts walking again. The knife went back into its sheath. I held my peace. Better so.

[1] A large, rounded earthenware container, seldom less and often more than 100 litres capacity, often used for the storage of wine and olive oil.

We moored out in the bay of Áyios Nikólaos, swam, rested at noon, and in the afternoon entered the harbour of Folégandros and walked up to the two-part village, one of the loveliest in all the Cyclades. In the evening we had home-baked bread, local wine, goat roasted over charcoal, garlic, a salad of tomatoes with onion, goat's-milk cheese, eggs fried in olive oil: our culture in its most enduring aspects. Gardening is of a piece with fishing, which is of a piece with architecture, which is of a piece with weaving, and all are of a piece with the religion, with the language, with the cycle of life and death, with heaven and earth. The ring is continuous: the ouroboros serpent. For me no other Cycladic village is like Folégandros, with its dignity, humility and spotless cleanliness (and most of them are similar). There are some houses and shops that stand out, some faces that are unforgettable, like the face of a certain fine-boned old woman wearing a headscarf, with violet eyes and girlish features, who asked me from the threshold of her house: 'Do you like our little island?' An island untouched, where moderation reigns in all things; a perfection that prefers to remain invisible, which does not even know that it is perfect, and which does not therefore merely possess knowledge but *is* knowledge. Blessed are they who have such secrets, and keep faith with the meaning of their life.

For what Heraclitus says about 'the limits of the soul' is also true of this life: 'such is the depth of its meaning', but at the same time such is this meaning's elusiveness, that it could be compared on the outside with the ratio of a circle's circumference to its diameter: the irrational and transcendental number $pi = 3.14159265$, which can never be fully grasped — in exactly the same way as the furthest reaches of the soul cannot be grasped, 'you could not discover [them] even if you travelled every path in order to do so'. And the meaning of this life is so profound and so elusive because the infinite cycle which determines it is also profound and elusive, the cycle which comes down from a point far distant in time and vanishes deep within man, linked to him through all those things which demonstrate his insecure place within creation, and which eternally guide him or make him one with the terrestrial, the chthonic and the heavenly simultaneously. We no longer reflect on these forms or commemorate these cycles. What then is the cycle which determines the meaning of the life of people on a Cycladic island like Folégandros? Let us be more clear as to what we are talking about.

This cycle takes its being from the boundless hinterland which opens before us — in the world outside as well as within — when we look at past centuries and ask ourselves where we come from, both actually and spiritually (this is a logical distinction, not a real one). According to the archaeologists, it appears that sometime around 7,000 BC in the valley of the Euphrates — and later of the Nile — agriculture (cultivation of wheat) and animal husbandry came into being for the first time, and these formed the general basis of the economies of both East and West, spreading from their place of origin, the so-called Middle East, eastwards and westwards to the Atlantic and Pacific shores, into Europe, India, Southeast Asia and the Far East. The whole of this world — and it is practically the whole world — has teemed ever since with the cosmologies, mythologies and rituals familiar to us today; broadly speaking, all the guiding principles and major themes, not just of mythology and religion, but of the ancient cosmologies and later of philosophy, were born there, and they spread, or rather were transmitted (through teaching and tradition) to all the great civilizations which developed in Europe, India, Southeast Asia and the Far East. The agricultural year with its rituals and its established festivals 'on earth',

and the cycle of the Zodiac 'in heaven', which was later divided (by astronomers in the region of the Euphrates) into
successive sections in accordance with the twelve annual
periods of the full moon — these had their beginning there,
both in place and in time, and ever since then they have reg-
ulated and also guided, in practical and spiritual terms, the
life of the great civilizations insofar as we know them. Obviously, in this cosmogonic nebula, as it were, nothing can be
clearly seen, and each of us must delve into his own tradition
in order to seek for the defining purpose of his life, and for
the Ariadne's thread that will help him to escape out of the
pandemonium of contemporary life, the confusion and the
Platonic 'ignorance' in which all of us are at sea.

For about 10,000 years — to be precise, almost 9,000, from
7,000 BC until now — it could be said that man has been living the agricultural phase of his life, with all the practical and
spiritual dimensions attendant upon this life both in place and
in time, linking, guiding and finally making man, physically
and metaphysically (a distinction not real but logical), one
with the earthly, the chthonic and the heavenly simultaneously. Heaven and earth, the world above and the world below,
became indissolubly linked with him and helped him create
civilizations which were in perfect correspondence (whether
their successive and disparate branches were at the peak of
their flowering or at the waning of their autumn, whether in
Europe or India, Southeast Asia or the Far East) with the stars
in the sky, the depths of the earth which were plumbed 'in the
sweat of [his] brow', as it says in the Book of Genesis, and in
harmony even with his own entrails which reflected inconceivable mysteries within him and provided conclusive replies
to questions concerning the cycle of life and death, light and
darkness, day and night, which, like Kálvos's spider, wrapped
him all around

With light and with death
unceasingly.

It must be said that these distinctions, like the one we are making now between agricultural as opposed to technological civilization, and any others, always define situations in a very rough, sketchy, simplistic way, much as in mathematics when we simplify a fraction, an equation or a formula, even though this does not alter their validity. (We all create our own patterns.) Nevertheless, they are useful in order to clarify what we are talking about; and if we accept that the pulley of Archytas (which we spoke of as being symbolic or representative in our first notebook), can effortlessly be included within the context of the almost ten thousand years that we have briefly described, and of the civilization that prevailed generally at the time, then the civilization which is now in the process of being formed, and whose representative symbol as opposed to Archytas's pulley is Edison's light bulb, is not only a civilization wholly other than those which have appeared up until now, but in addition is, I would say, a different world altogether. In our years, technology, whether or not that was its intention, is well on the way to destroying everywhere the systems which — as we said — were initially based on agriculture and animal husbandry, in East and West, and to abandon both them and the ancient cosmologies, philosophical visions, religions and myths, as well as the question which is of most moment for the whole world, physically and metaphysically: what for man constitutes the 'best life', as the Greeks formulated it. And it has not set out to destroy these systems alone, but every system or vision like them which has sustained smaller groups of human beings within the world, from the jungle to the steppe and from the savannah to the tundra. It will not succeed. The spiritual seed of tradition is well protected within its shell, and also, of course, within man. If technological civilization in the course of its progress — whether this will be long or short we do not know — oversteps those difficult limits which the agricultural civilization knew as 'measure', μέτρα in Greek (whether by doing physical damage or metaphysical harm), we can be sure that the Erinyes, 'the handmaidens of justice', will find the transgressor, track him down, and stop him. This law, one of the great themes of an age-old spirituality, has always functioned on all levels, for it was formulated not only in the Greek world around 500 BC by Heraclitus and the Tragedians, but before them by the Hebrews in the Psalms: 'Thou hast set a bound that they may not pass over' and in the Proverbs: 'Remove not the ancient landmark, that thy fathers have set'. Today, global thermal pollution,[1] the great unacknowledged danger, and the ugliness in general of most of the works of technological civilization (in art for example), which increasingly threaten both our inner and outer life, testify everywhere to the ill omens which have dogged this civilization from its beginning, a civilization which has fantasized about space when it should have been attending to its own

---

[1] The present text does not require footnotes, apart from the odd reference here and there. Nevertheless, for the reader's information, I quote from an unpublished (or more precisely unfinished) writing of mine the following estimation by someone who knows, 'di color che sanno' as Dante would say, and which would seem almost prophetically related to what is being said here: 'Present emission of energy is about $1/15,000$ of the absorbed solar flux. But if the present rate of growth continued for 250 years emissions would reach 100% of the absorbed solar flux. The resulting increase in the earth's temperature would be about 50°C — a condition totally unsuitable for human habitation.' (L. R. Heilbroner, 'The Human Prospect', *New York Review of Books*, 24th January 1974). The hypothetical 250 year deadline makes so-called global thermal pollution at the moment more of a warning than a threat. The quotation says it all.

affairs and to what was taking place in front of its nose — exactly like the wise Thales whom Socrates derided in the *Theaetetus* for being '... so eager to know what was happening in the sky that he could not see what lay at his feet' and 'when he was looking up to study the stars [he] tumbled down a well'. The only difference being that today there exists the fear that the well may be big enough not just for Thales, but for all of us.

I was saying that technological civilization will not succeed in destroying the spiritual seed. The categorical nature of this opinion is based, among other things, on those exceptional people, of whom there are not a few, who live within this civilization yet lose no opportunity to sound the alarm every time any serious threats to the 'measure' we were speaking of appear on the horizon, or when 'during moments of intense study', as Cavafy* says,

> *the hidden sound*
> *of things approaching reaches them.*

But it is also based on the widespread admiration inspired by those monuments of art and literature which have been above all concerned to glorify most vividly, one might say, man's mystical bond with creation and its creator — for example, the universal attitude of awe of contemporary Europeans before the cathedrals built by their forefathers in the Middle Ages — and on the nostalgia felt by most people for that longed-for wholeness, so to speak, as opposed to the inhuman disjunction, the fragmentation of technological civilization — the longing for the unbroken ring of life which one encounters in the Cycladic islands and in places where that precious spiritual possession still exists and people still hang on to it (many of them without realizing it), keeping faith with the meaning of their lives. Technology may have achieved unheard-of things in a spectacularly short space of time, it may have accomplished things in that time which have not been accomplished in the preceding 9,000 years, it may have afforded man better protection from illness, bodily pain, bad weather (both cold and hot), physical labour, difficult times; it may have furnished him with innumerable comforts, abolished or shortened distances, doled out impersonally various conveniences, asphalted over the forests and penetrated the mountains and dried out swampland and planted the desert, but with the uncontrolled increase in production it has used up the reserves of continents and oceans to a dangerous degree, provoked an explosion in the population of the earth, polluted the atmosphere, the land and the sea along with their produce, damaged (and in many places annihilated) flora and fauna, and has artificially generated needs without improving the quality of life or bringing man happiness. Despite all these incredible achievements, the problem of happiness remains as uncompromisingly unresolved as it ever was. Places like Folégandros teach us about our origins and set the dilemma in its true perspective. We must either subject technological civilization to the guiding principles and main lines of conduct followed for almost 9,000 years by all those systems which bound man closely to creation and its creator, stopping the upward curve of production and the downward curve of waste (unlimited development and limited resources don't go together; time has passed and the hour of reckoning has arrived); or we will destroy ourselves, and in doing so, there is the risk that with us in our fall will go this favoured planet, which was given to us, as we are told in the Book of Genesis, to inhabit from the day that 'God said, Let us make man'.

We are speaking very generally, in broad simplistic terms. Nevertheless, we are not so very far from the truth. At this point the (newer) West should take a look at the (older) East, and rather than ignore it, should approach it and seek out the points of contact — they still exist — which used at one time to link these two worlds together, without touching on the striking differences between them (one does not rule out the other). On that day the dilemma will be favourably resolved, and then it is likely that Goethe's dictum will be fulfilled, in which he said that East and West should no longer be separated:

> *Orient und Occident*
> *Sind nicht mehr zu trennen.*

Until then what is needed is patience and love for both East and West. And the realization that sometimes we find help where we don't expect to (as we don't hear the bullet being fired which ends up in our body).

With their food, their fishing, their gardening, their weaving, their architecture, with their music and songs, their language, their religion, their fields and their sea, with the cycle of their life attuned to the progress of the sun and the constellations in the firmament, with their tools and their trades, the inhabitants of Folégandros teach us a strange lesson which inexplicably touches the depths of the contemporary traveller, both the passer-by and the sojourner. We must therefore originate from somewhere, if we patiently start to spell out the different patterns and cycles which we have so briefly and hastily alluded to. And finally we will have to ask ourselves outright the decisive question. We city people, with so much knowledge in our heads — but without true knowledge, as it appears — confronted with these islanders who, as we said, do not simply possess knowledge but *are* knowledge, who possess nothing because they are capable of possessing everything (without knowing it) — do we accomplish anything more than these people accomplish, in spite of all the amazing labours of the new Hercules of technological culture, up to the moment when both of us will hear the final pronouncement: 'The earth is the Lord's and the fulness thereof'? Death has no place in the culture of technology. Yet the poet of another culture, Francisco Quevedo (1580–1645), in his marvellous *Poemas metafísicos*, makes a comparison (which I include here, since we are crossing seas and hauling on sails), an image of death, which man stumbles across quite casually and the whole situation changes in an instant, 'comes one fell stroke, and Death in turn prevails over all these vanities', without anyone having the time to realize what is actually happening:

> *Like him who sails joyfully over the sea,*
> *And, himself unmoving, flies with the wind,*
> *And before he thinks of arriving, has arrived.*

Or, in Quevedo's own words:

> *Como el que, divertido, el mar navega,*
> *y, sin moverse, vuela con el viento,*
> *y antes que piense en acercare, llega.*

So much for the great symbolic wholes. We are not talking about misplaced sentimental feelings or passing attractions towards those who live in the so-called paradise of some Aegean island, especially as we know how unrelenting towards man in this paradise are the land and the sea. If we leave the great wholes and think about the small part which is our country today, we can arrive at certain conclusions, not static and unmoving conclusions, but rather indications which point us, even in the dark, in the best possible direction. The point is not to confine oneself to a nostalgic lament — even when this is impressively or strongly expressed — for a way of life which is either vanishing or is in the process of adaptation, but to discover the enduring values of a country (of every country), the particular 'possession for all time' (Thucydides) of our spiritual culture, and not to retreat unthinkingly before the recent 'inexorable flood', as Solomós would say (which, along with a few good things, brings with it an immeasurable amount of junk), while at the same time working out the most appropriate method of crossing over to the new ways of life, which of course cannot be put off with impunity. I am not talking about those who would like to change everything and send the whole lot sky-high, nor of those who feel no nostalgia for anything in the past, who are attached to nothing, like blocks of wood. And I am not talking, either, about those who don't want anything changed, who bury themselves alive, as Pausanias was buried by his fellow countrymen at Sparta. These are two pointless categories of human being: both are always bigoted, always ranting, and always 'full of passionate intensity', as Yeats put it. A real disaster for the rest of us, in fact 'the worst', as the poet says. The former accept, unquestioningly or fanatically, everything that is alien. The latter, again unquestioningly or fanatically, accept nothing whatsoever. And the former don't change this mentality even when it comes to politics, where the local reality is visible in all its nakedness. 'Anglicisers... Frenchifiers... Russianisers', as Makriyánnis said a century ago. We do the same a century later. And the latter behave in exactly the same way. But just as you cannot *not* have a shell around you, neither can you shut yourself up in it. With the obvious proviso that any localized culture needs to grow wings and be helped, rather than deformed, by the different influences coming in from outside. Only by adopting this positive course of action can you actually improve for yourself the few good things that — as we said — come to you, among the unreckonable detritus which goes through the mill. The ancients apparently managed to do this, according to the assertion in Plato's *Epinomis*: 'Whenever Greeks borrow anything from non-Greeks, they finally carry it to a higher perfection.' If you are uncritical you can't even take in properly what is good, let alone protect yourself from what is bad. In our country, it is clear that the biggest noise and the greatest harm are created by the two categories of human being we have been speaking of, who do not conform to the law of life, who want either everything or nothing, neglecting all measure. This reveals many things, first and foremost among them being our abysmal ignorance concerning both the new things that we wish uncritically to import into our own lives (mostly with no more knowledge of them than what we have been able to pick up second-hand), and the old things that we want to throw out. Thus the baby is thrown out with the bath-water (and we sometimes go with it), and in the end we neither acquire what is good nor get rid of the bad, but the contrary. We flail around helplessly and destroy the innocent country (any country). In the case of many people in this country today, it is clear that in both body and soul they are closer to Moscow or London than to Alonístena or the Zagóri. They continue passively in a particular framework of thought, the product of particular circumstances in particular countries, and within which they enclose the life of their own country, whether or not it fits and whether or not it needs to go into the said framework. In the end they establish absolute modes of thinking in the place of relative modes of behaviour, or they sow and reap the intransigence of those who, like hypochondriacs, are afraid of draughts and never leave the windows of the house open. Given these habits, how will we ever get 'civilization in the village', as Papadiamándis ironically put it, and get it right? Furthermore, it is only the worst types of people or the most submissive who have acquired these habits of mind. Never, as Seféris* says somewhere, 'did it occur to the best to be afraid of foreigners to the extent of building walls to shut them out.' You cannot turn your back on today's technological culture (and the western philosophy which lies behind it) and ignore it, but you can study it without feelings of inferiority, and judge or condemn it — as is your right — not for its few good things, but on the points which have effectively convinced you, after serious study, that this civilization as it now stands constitutes a deadly threat to the possibility of living an acceptable life, to that which in ancient philosophy, we say it for one last time, was seen as man's ultimate aim, and which it called the best life. Especially since now it is not just 'the best' that is in danger (for man), but the 'life' itself as well.

I am writing these self-evident things because every so often in this country we hear rumours (not well-founded, it is true, but presented mainly in newspapers, journalistic criticism and ephemeral magazines) of a certain attitude towards these problems which has been christened 'hellenocentric'. This is a jargon-derived word whose true meaning I have never been able to grasp, and which can only be properly understood, it seems, by those who speak the jargon, rather as in the old days the tinkers of Épirus or the gypsies of Karpeníssi had a language of their own. As in the case of the previous examples, I believe that the correct answer to this so-called 'hellenocentrism' is clearly provided by the above-mentioned remark of Seféris regarding 'the best', and that is the end of it. For the others, i.e. the worst, there is no need of further engagement with non-existent problems and of multiplying to no purpose, in this country of ours, the scholastics' *entia ... praeter necessitatem* ['entities should not be multiplied beyond necessity', William of Occam, c.1285–1349]. I consider that this attitude (we have called it an attitude) of 'hellenocentrism', along with that other attitude or exhortation or catchword of the 'return'— any kind of return — to somewhere or anywhere (yet another non-existent problem, given that — as Heraclitus says — you can never step twice into the same river) and the alternative tendency seen in some people to run headlong after some invariably golden future, must both be steadily and consistently excluded from any serious discussion, as a waste of time.

But let us re-emerge into the sea air. And let us not forget, out here where the summer sun gilds the world, the fragment by Pindar which says that there exists, among various other sorts of people, the man who rejoices in being carried safely along over the waves in a swift ship. This man seems to have existed from the dawn of time, and his joyous journey does not seem to resemble any modern situation or any contemporary mind-set.

15th, Sunday. Síkinos.

16th. We left before dawn for Irakleiá. Out at sea we passed Iós, leaving its northern cape, Áspros Gremós, on our right, and at noon we moored in Schinoússa's protected harbour, Mersiniá. We changed our plans, seeing that we were in a protected anchorage and that the weather, even though it is June, looks as though it will turn windy.

17th, Tuesday. Antikéri (Greater and Lesser).

St George of Antikéri
Whitened shell per lo gran mar dell'essere
Joining our own sea
At the point where the land falls apart,
From your severe and patient icon
Bend down a little, cover us — like the bucket
Left upended on the wooden cover of your cistern...

We left, hugging the coast around Kéros, and spent one more night on Schinoússa.

18th. In the morning we hopped over to Irakleiá, with its small deep harbour, long and narrow, exposed to the north-easterly wind. A little before noon we set out for the Koufoníssia, where we went for a long walk. Even though the inhabited Koufoníssi is a large fishing centre in the region, it also has animals and a thriving agriculture (as have Schinoússa and Irakleiá to a greater extent), along with a beauty and a quality of land and sea (let alone light) which I find impossible to describe — not because I might not manage to do so with a middling or even a fair degree of success, not because I don't esteem the act of writing, but because to a much greater degree I esteem life itself, and I believe that its essence is always grasped through living it and never through writing about it. (I say to myself that herein may lie the secret meaning of my own name.*) In writing, you are simply chewing over the rind of life. And yet, there are times — thank God there are only a few of them — where I confess that I violate this principle of mine. For this reason, most of my few writings are not about life (life cannot be written) but about study. And they are almost never descriptions or definitions, which to my mind are vanity. To define means to limit. We can ascertain this linguistically in Latin, where the word *definitio* and the word *limitatio* have the same meaning. I wonder whether, at the end of the day, there exists a real conflict between art and life, between living and writing, or is the problem perhaps a pseudo-problem? I think not, and that there is a conflict — an unbridgeable gulf. And I think that this may well be what the Elizabethan poet Ben Jonson so effectively described as 'all the adulteries of art', in a song which ends with the sublime lines:

> *Give me a book, give me a face*
> *That makes simplicity a grace,*
> *Robes loosely flowing, hair as free,*
> *Such sweet neglect more taketh me*
> *Than all the adulteries of art;*
> *They strike mine eyes, but not my heart.*

It is particularly on those occasions when we confuse the relationship between them, mostly as a result of theorizing (for in actuality, since all who write, necessarily live, and those who live don't necessarily write, the relationship is not confused), that the problem is more evident: when art seeks to become in some way 'more philosophical and a higher thing' than life, to stand above life or to confront it and examine it, which is what happened with Descartes' famous philosophical inversion, when *cogito* was put before *sum*, writing (*o altra cosa* *) before living, art before life, the word before the spirit — a fatal conflict which brought technological civilization into diametrical opposition with all the previous civilizations referred to above. (When we look at the monuments of art and see the abysmal change for the worse which broadly speaking divides the past from the present, we can speak of the cultures of *sum* and *cogito* respectively.) A civilization guided by Descartes' philosophical inversion will inevitably end up where technology is today, unless life and thought, *sum* and *cogito*, become one, or rather unless our thought has become one with life, as in the following illuminating extract from a letter written by Joseph Conrad to a friend on February 8th 1899: 'J'ai jeté ma vie à tous les vents du ciel mais j'ai gardé ma pensée. C'est peu de chose — c'est tout — ce n'est rien — c'est la vie même.' These are the words of someone who does not think his thoughts but lives his thoughts, and thinks his life. And the Cartesian example puts one in mind of Wittgenstein's fly, which, not content with pondering on how to get out of the bottle (no other civilization has ever set such a goal — 'Ziel' — for philosophy), attempts, with the help of Descartes, to convince us that the bottle in which 'we live and move and have our being' (to use St Paul's phrase) is second in importance to the fly. The relevant passage is in the *Philosophische Untersuchungen* (I, 309), addressed to the philosopher, and you may take it as you please: 'What is your goal in philosophy? To show the fly the way out of its bottle.' ('Was ist dein Ziel in der Philosophie? — Der Fliege den Ausweg aus dem Fliegenglas zeigen.')

I was saying that the essence is grasped through living, not through writing. I was also saying that I might be able, in some fashion, to undertake descriptions, with a middling or even acceptable result. I might. I will now add to my few violations of my rule by attempting, out of sheer love, a description of the little place by the sea that I have known since childhood and where I still go when I make my pilgrimage to the island where I was born and where I belong. I try and go to this place mainly when I am there in early spring or late autumn, when people have gone away.

* * *

At the place I am talking about, the village is about a quarter of an hour's walk away and cannot be seen from the bay.

If one continues on to where the shadowy olive groves come to an end, one arrives at the edge of a cliff which goes down to the sea. The place is all rocks. The little path gets damaged during the winter by the heavy rains which bring down mud and clay, and every summer the villagers repair it at certain points so as to be able to pass along it. In order to get down to the bay you take the right-hand fork. The left-hand fork leads to a small vegetable patch planted with courgettes, tomatoes and beans and terraced on two or three descending levels, each of them enclosed on the seaward side by rows of canes, with a small trickle of water among the maidenhair ferns growing on the rock. There are spiny aloes in all directions, standing guard over the entire area. If you go along the path to the bay in early spring, before it has been trodden by anyone, you will come to a sudden stop before a slippery crossing of earth buried under masses of weeds and wildflowers, where you need to calculate every step of your dangerous and difficult progress. In some places the undergrowth and grasses are practically head-high, and you are in a scented and magical place full of wild mint, butterflies and the first swallows. Up to the point where the path starts to descend towards the bottom of the cliff, it is an incredible experience. The whole cliff resembles a sanctuary of which man's presence is a violation and a desecration, and it is as though everything, from the bushes and tall grasses to the rainbow-coloured insects and birds which fly to and fro unceasingly, is all aquiver because someone has seen them at the wrong moment, has surprised them, like a young virgin, at the secret moment of their nakedness. The path gets wider as you go down and you can continue with comparative ease to the rocks at the end of the bay.

There, suddenly, unexpectedly, concealed from view, remote and unlooked-for from a few steps away, on your right as you stop facing the sea, is a little hidden sandy beach, or rather a shell of sand, a tiny patch (I liken it to the proportions of the ancient theatre of Amphiárion, that hidden jewel of a place near Oropós), lying within a hollow in the cliffs and encircled by high pointed rocks which emerge several metres above the sea like the masts of ships. Here the downward path ends. No words can describe this sand, its each and every grain. You have to have walked on it and to have had the rare privilege, in early spring or in late autumn when there are no people, of bathing in the unruffled blue water which inhabits it and washes it night and day, in order properly to take the measure of such a gift. Otherwise, both you the reader and I the writer are working to no purpose. The sand extends into deep water, and to the right the landscape is completed by a barren height and by a double cave chiselled out of the rock — Homer's σπέος γλαφυρό or hollow cave, home to the sea-goddesses Thetis and Eurynome. Another thing which makes you unable to take your eyes off this little shell of sand is its irresistible proportions, which I've already mentioned, its treasure-trove of light, and the contrast it presents to the towering dark blue mountain of the island — like a smile confronting a scowl — which at that point casts its massive shadow to the far horizon, and which the islanders, appropriately enough, name Megálo Vounó, the Big Mountain. Supposing that someone were to seek for the inevitable metaphor in order to make the transition from nature to art and back to nature, there is one line alone capable of capturing the correspondence between the two worlds of nature and art in this place: the magic phrase by Gérard de Nerval, who was known to his fellow-countrymen as 'le fol délicieux' (as indeed he was):

J'ai rêvé dans la grotte où nage la sirène…

This place invokes the exterior sense of the line, and the line invokes the inner sense of the place, in the closest possible approximation, in a context where we should never expect to find total identification.

* * *

With regard to the standard metaphor linking nature to art and back again, we have T. S. Eliot's famous theory of the 'objective correlative', which has reference to approximation rather than to identification. It is worth observing the working-out of Eliot's scheme.

In 1910 Ezra Pound wrote in *The Spirit of Romance*: 'Poetry is a sort of inspired mathematics, which give us... equations for the human emotions.'

In 1917, T. S. Eliot, in *Ezra Pound: His Metric and Poetry*, quotes the following remark by F. M. Ford (1873–1939): 'Poetry consists in so rendering concrete objects that the emotions produced by the objects shall arise in the reader...'.

Finally, in 1919, Eliot notes in 'Hamlet and his Problems': 'The only way of expressing emotion in the form of art is by finding an "objective correlative"; in other words, a set of objects, a situation, a chain of events which shall be the formula of that particular emotion; such that when the external facts, which must terminate in sensory experience, are given, the emotion is immediately evoked.'

The word 'emotion' is the key to all three texts. Eliot's 'objective correlative' has the variant 'objective equivalent' — a little later in the same essay — and 'objective equivalents' in a later essay of his, 'Cyril Tourneur' (1931). Anyone who is interested in going more deeply into the subject can find out more about it in the lecture given by Eliot in 1961 and entitled 'To Criticize the Critic', along with priceless autobiographical information and explanations relating to his poetic and critical writings in general. Whoever is not interested, on the other hand, can confine themselves to the practical approximation of nature and art and ignore this theoretical section, which follows the successive stages of Eliot's 'objective correlative'.

* * *

19th, Thursday. We raised the sail late in the day and went to the bay of Kalandó on Náxos, with its long sandy beach. We continued in the afternoon and stopped in the evening, far out, at Aï-Yánni (still Náxos) for the night. The humidity was tropical.

20th. We left in the morning for Vathí, on Sífnos, in bad weather, cloudy with a north-east wind, and a swell. At 3.30 in the afternoon we dropped anchor. There was a wonderful little chapel dedicated to the Archangels Michael and Gabriel and two or three clay ovens. A strong westerly wind got up which lasted all night and only died down towards dawn.

Saturday 21st. We set out for Kamáres [Sífnos] (where we spent the night) and went round the island. In the afternoon the west wind got up again, which at this season of the year is known hereabouts as the *koufonótia*.

22nd. We left Sífnos with a north-westerly wind, at 8.30. At 6.30 in the afternoon we anchored off Kolóna at Thermiá [Kíthnos], behind the chapel of St Luke, not far from Mérika. We had been tossed about all day. This was followed by a dead calm, the day before the full moon. The cycle was complete.

23rd, Monday, the Feast of the Holy Spirit, we set out on the return journey at 6 a.m., leaving Tziá [Kéa] on our right, and around 3 o'clock in the afternoon we anchored in Glifáda.

As we passed Tziá, we could see in the distance on the dim horizon of Athens the menacing cloud which we were shortly to enter, and, given the places we were coming from, this 'system' out of the Apocalypse, spreading for miles from its furnaces up into one of the world's most dazzling skies, seemed even more hideous and filthy. We had been living in God's world and were now returning into the world of man, into the world that man — a certain type of man — is in the process of creating. In other words, we were leaving the culture of *sum* and entering the culture of *cogito*.

Away in the small islanded archipelago below Náxos we could see, traced in an arc of transparency, a single, almost uninterrupted, continuous line of human activity, despite all the great variations within each particular period, starting with the men of the fishing caiques today and going back to the Cretan or Cycladic ships captained by 'men with archaic pointed beards' (as in the drawings on ancient pots) which are nostalgically recalled, and rightly so, in the poem 'The Greeks are Coming' by D. H. Lawrence, himself the son of a coal-miner steeped in the coal-dust of Nottingham. And at this point I call to mind a pertinent observation made by the Greek scholar D. F. Kitto, to which no one has paid any attention over the years, as far as I am aware: 'The simple fact that no ancient civilization had coal has not, I think, been sufficiently considered by social historians' (*The Greeks*, ch. 3, 1951). I would add that, apart from the social historians, the question is worth consideration from others also, the philosophers and anthropologists and lastly (or firstly) the poets. The observation is a very far-reaching one.

I was saying how away in that little archipelago we saw human activity taking place within an arc of transparency.

Here we will soon be unable to see anything at all. We do not know how long the 'system', which I have described as out of the Apocalypse because it brings man up against hitherto unknown perspectives and 'great signs', will last (we know it won't last for ever) but — to express it as an oxymoron — this transitoriness seems like finality while it is still going on or developing, and it does not allow man to reflect that the specific philosophy and the general mentality which gave rise to the system and which appear for most people to be all-powerful (although there are quite a number of dissenting voices) will pass away someday, will depart, and all that will remain will be the acquisitions or the good things procured for man by the incredible achievements which were realized in the spectacularly short space of one century, as we said above, with the exception of the two goals that are increasingly becoming the subject of discussion: quality of life (which has not improved) and happiness (which has not been found). Providing, of course, that no irreversible cosmic disaster takes place in the meantime.

To take members of the upper class and intellectuals from the various centres, whether as state appointees or private businesses — lawyers, economists, architects, civil engineers, technicians, contractors, designers, decorators or pseudo-artists, well-travelled or less so — put them on one of the small remoter islands such as Irakleiá, and allow them to practise their professions there in accordance with their studies and their general culture, as they have done in the capital and in all the major Greek cities, as well as in the villages (which inevitably imitate the big cities) with the consequences familiar to us all — this would be an act of arrogance, a downright insult showing ignorant contempt for a people who have remained so remarkably in harmony with the spirit and the letter of this country in all aspects of life, under the most relentless circumstances of slavery or dislocation, whether foreign or native. I say this because I do not consider it necessary for each and every corner of land and sea in Greece, including places like Irakleiá and the Koufoníssia, to be a faithful copy of the big cities during their transition from a farming society (with sailors and fishermen) to an urban and industrial society. Just because a society like that of Greece today is rapidly changing from the agricultural life to one of urbanization and industrialization, it does not follow that it must sell its soul to the devil or lose its mind altogether, to the extent that nothing is left of the ancient traditions which have passed unscathed through far greater events and experienced countless drastic changes. So far we have been watching the game of how a country of great vitality adapts itself to some of the requirements of the new era, characterized first and foremost by the absence of any sense of direction about where we come from or where we are going, culturally speaking, and with a whole series of premature beginnings with no end, or with plans which change by the week, like the moon. The game needs care in the playing. And there is no need for things to go wrong everywhere. When the entire country is destroyed, what is going on is no longer a game but something extremely serious. It is what the architect Pikiónis* called in his pastoral language 'dishonouring the earth'. (When I say 'pastoral' I am not speaking rhetorically; I mean 'referring to the spiritual shepherd'.) The swarms of educated people whom I momentarily envisaged being set loose on Irakleiá, with their studies and their cultural know-how, to transform it within a few days from underdeveloped to developed (and no one has told us, incidentally, how they reckon development) is not just an imaginary scenario, but a *fait accompli* in many places with no justification. It is as though their very education leaves the ruling classes and the educated people dangling, and they lose touch altogether with real things and the power of real things, like Antaeus as soon as he was lifted off the earth. I don't know what it is that happens to them with their education, but I do know that something happens and that they are transformed in the end into a race of barbarians. If we judge by the results, we have to agree that most of the works which take place each day in the bigger and the smaller cities, and not only the cities, are totally opposed to the cultural heritage of the country — I don't mean the classical or the Byzantine heritage, but whatever heritage it is that makes us what we are — and are opposed also to certain inner laws operative within the man who is native to a place, and to certain external laws of heaven and earth, land and sea, which make one place distinct from another and condemn to spiritual failure or collapse anyone who 'oversteps the measure' appropriate to each place. The people have respected these laws in all aspects of their life, and have paid homage, with works which are simple and unaffected, to a unique physical environment, land and sea, heaven and earth, with which they have always remained in harmony, both in freedom and in slavery, in good times as in bad. This is what we have totally betrayed. Instead of using education as a means of understanding our cultural make-up, as a means to develop its capacity to adapt to a new reality (which in its turn will have to adapt to yet another one, in accordance with the law of life, so that the old can be revitalized by the new and the new stabilized by the old, whereas now it emerges from its swaddling-clothes disabled and discordant, as Papadiamándis would say), we have confined ourselves to our studies and have turned our cultural heritage into a *tabula rasa*. Whenever we do make use of it, it is as an ornamental or aesthetic element, decorative rather than functional, in other words pointless. Educated people, riding the well-nourished horse of education, look down their noses at their ancestral heritage — the spiritual virtue that Makriyánnis called 'a most precious jewel, which we held on to under the Turkish yoke'; they all want to lead the people instead of being led by them, and, believing themselves to be important and famous, always presume to teach the people whose life is one of anonymity. Some want the people to unlearn their language, others want them to unlearn their faith. They want to teach them how they ought to speak and what they should believe so as to be able to copy them, they want them to be delivered to them bound hand and foot so as to get them to be like their lordships, and one day to become as good as them. And they forget that the higher a monkey climbs, the more clearly you see its backside. When we say that we are our country's worst enemy, we are saying no more than that man's worst enemy is man himself. And when we ask who will save our country from itself (which at present is us), it is like asking who will save man from himself. For us this is a local problem, but at the same time it is a universal human problem in every place. The goal of all spiritual traditions, as opposed to the newer philosophical systems which dream up external solutions, has always been to solve this problem, to save man from man. 'I have not come to judge…but to save', says Christ in the Gospel of John. The result is decided on two levels, spiritual and philosophical, spirit and letter. One is life, the other is study. *Sum* and *cogito*: between them, separating them, is a yawning abyss.

Man's feelings about the world and the state, and his feelings regarding creation and God, ought not to be identified or confused with each other. There must be priority and precedence. In our day the overturning of all values,

Nietzsche's Umwertung aller Werte [transvaluation of all values], has resulted in mass derangement, exemplified in the famous statement: 'What times are these...' ('Was sind das für Zeiten...') of Bertold Brecht, a poet who deplores our times because it seems almost a crime, for his political conscience, to be talking about trees when there are so many abominations waiting to be uncovered in society. (As if the abominations had appeared for the first time in our days, or as if this was the first time man had tried to correct them.) The thinking is topsy-turvy. In the case in question it is poetry (the poet being the man, apparently, who talks about trees) which is made to take the blame, while at the same time we see how our attempts to correct or change the many abominations of society as we uncover them, frequently results in abominations even greater than before, if that were possible. It is often the case that the cure does us greater harm than the illness itself. The 20th century is full of such examples. Why should poetry be put in the dock? And why, on top of that, should we be burdened with a guilty conscience? There is no precedence or priority. Poetry, rather than politics, is found guilty, for example, priority being assigned to man's feelings about the world and the state, when we have irrevocably polluted creation and squander its resources like a spendthrift street-walker. Where, then, do we rate man's feelings for creation or for God? Do they come before or after the others? What takes precedence for us or has more significance on our list when we reflect on man's position in the cosmos: the first nightingale song heard amidst God's creation in springtime, or a piece of legislation from the state? Which is the spirit and which the letter? And which comes first in this context, the spirit or the letter? *Sum* or *cogito*? It makes no sense.

So, in order not to confuse man's feelings about the world

or the state with his feelings about creation or God, and so as not to identify them with each other, you must choose which is the spirit and which the letter, which pole star is going to shine in your inner sky and guide your steps on earth, so that you look upwards — within yourself — before beginning to do things on earth (whether in relation to the world or the state, creation or God), and so that the things you do are done 'on earth as it is in heaven', as the Lord's Prayer enjoins. Otherwise, you will be looking for heaven on earth, and for earth in heaven, and you won't find either the one where it isn't or the other where it is. You will be left dangling.

Civilizations are judged according to their works.

THIRD NOTEBOOK 1976

11th June (Friday). We set out in the morning, not very early. In the evening we arrived at Thermiá [Kíthnos], at Fykáda, under a full moon. All day we had been almost continuously under sail.

12th. We passed north of Sérifos and anchored off Chersónissos, Sífnos (Áyios Giórgios on the map). It was a fine day. We passed Pipéri and Serfopoúla on our left and on our right the rock known as Vous, close to Sérifos, in the second strait between Sérifos and Sífnos (the first is between Thermiá and Sérifos).

13th. We left Chersónissos, and the wonderful church of St Philip on the crest of the mountain, with its blue dome and its three-columned bell-tower. We passed to the north of the island, very far out to sea, heading for the north side of Páros (Náoussa). A huge swordfish leapt high into the air twice on our right, out of the unruffled sea. Summer has arrived.

A school of unusually large dolphins appeared all round us in the middle of the strait.

We doubled the lighthouse of Cape Kóraka in the late afternoon and entered Náoussa harbour. We had a swim in the crystal-clear blue-green water off St John's, whose bells were ringing for evening prayer.

14th. Set out for Cape Stavrós on Náxos, approaching it from the north side. We used the motor and only a little sail. In the middle of the trip, dolphins came around us in twos, threes and fours, big and little. From a distance the chain formed by their successive leaps one after the other out of the sea resembles the turning of a windmill's sails. Their gracefulness is indescribable, inconceivable:

> *And all your reckoning ends in nothing*
> *As though you were counting waves or stars*

In the afternoon we anchored at Stavrós, Donoússa. Virgin sand, water like sky; had a swim.

15th. Went for a ride in the boat as far as Kéndro, the next beach along. Swimming, lunch, sun. We went on as far as Vathí Limenári, and anchored again at Kámbos, or Stavrós. There are a hundred inhabitants on Donoússa (which the older generation pronounce Denoússa), fifty at Stavrós and the rest scattered around at Mersíni, Messariá and further away at Kalotaritíssa and the island of Skyloníssi opposite, not far from the north lighthouse of the island.

16th. Today I went for a walk by myself to Vathí Limenári. I think that the few ancient ruins that exist there belonged to a community like the Cycladic communities of Amorgós and Kéros. The villagers told me that some of them have found 'little dolls' made of marble (what archaeologists call statuettes). The island is all stones and cliffs, yet it has a beauty similar to that of the Koufoníssia or to Schinoússa which is level. Blessed places in the 'great might', as Pericles said, of the eternal sea. I swam again at Kéndro, and someone took me back from there in his boat (we met by chance as I was strolling around). I got to Stavrós in the afternoon.

Tomorrow we're thinking of setting sail for Lévitha. (I have met a beautiful old woman here who has forty-four grandchildren. Her eyes were like the eyes of that other wonderfully gracious old woman last year on Folégandros.)

Suddenly in the evening, in just a few minutes, a local south-westerly wind blew up which comes from the direction of the Mákares, some deserted islands behind Náxos, and lays everything flat. The smaller boats were hastily dragged up onto the sand and we left immediately for Kalotarítissa, to find protection on the other side of the island. As we approached, we saw the majestic Cape Tebélis, with the island's lighthouse on its northern edge. Wild and majestic. We entered, leaving Skyloníssi on our left. At midnight the anchor came loose and we re-anchored further out, adding a second one. Violent gusts of wind came off the sides of Pápa and Várdia, the two mountains. This went on all night and into the morning.

17th of the month: one element dominates, Kálvos's

> *I hear the mad raging*
> *Of the wind.*

You may say to me: You put it like that because you have a bit of education. Be that as it may, this element dominates everyone, whether or not they are educated. But to describe this island in words (*o altra cosa**) is to ruin it. It's better to live it. To learn and to be silent.

We spent all day at Kalotarítissa, inhabited since neolithic times. Once again I realize that the farmer and the fisherman are the alpha and the omega of this land, and its true aristocracy. The rest of us are just variations or rather distortions of these two original cells. It's a failure whenever anyone distances himself from the laws of the place, certain inexpressible laws, or when he tries to export the forms which are native to the place to a different locale. This is the failure of those who have attempted to reproduce ancient Greek civilization, one of the greatest in the world, according to the letter rather than the spirit. It will be the failure, sooner or later, of all those who do not respect the laws of the place as its first inhabitants respected them. And what appears strange, even though it isn't, is the fact that the same laws do not mean that what is produced is always the same. In the course of time we do not see stagnation, in fact the contrary is true. The spirit changes the letter and bloweth where it listeth.

18th. We left for Lévitha, setting a course of 100°. Soon we saw strings of dolphins in the morning mist. Dead calm, the sea like oil. There was a wonderful estate on the island, enclosed by stone walls like those in Scotland (which I've seen) or Ireland (which I haven't seen), or perhaps in the Aran Islands (which I dream about). Two brothers with their wives and children were the owners. And there were fishing caiques coming and going continually — from Kálymnos, Pátmos, Léros, Foúrnous, Ikariá and elsewhere. A veritable centre of various intersecting maritime activities, reprehensible and not. We spent one night there tied up in the south harbour (there is a western one as well). Running before the north wind you can get from Lévitha to Astropaliá [Astypálaia]. God willing, we will leave for there tomorrow.

19th. We set out for Astropaliá, setting a course of 180°. We were buffeted about by the waves for quite a long while and reached the island on a peaceful Saturday afternoon. When we entered, there was a very strong north wind and squalls. Cape Poúlaris gave us hell as we rounded it. High above Skála, the new houses have tamed the castle over the centuries. There was light coming from everywhere, almost like the spiritual 'light of evening' that our Church celebrates in one of its hymns at Vespers (and it was that hour of the day, too).

On the other side of the island is little Livádi with its market gardens, and nearer at hand, on the ridge or rather the watershed of the mountain, near the Kástro, are nine windmills in a row, which today's fifty-somethings still remember grinding corn. Now they no longer grind, and are crumbling away; they remind one of the demotic song:

> *Mother with your nine good sons and with your single*
> *daughter.*

The island is the mother; the sons are the mills. And who is the one daughter, faithful and eternal, who never crumbles and never fails, who is not overtaken by death like her brothers, but who herself is capable of destroying? She, perhaps, is the all-encircling sea.

Sunday 20th June and Monday 21st. We are stuck here because of the weather. We do the round of the island. It looks as if we'll be here for longer, who knows how long. Gazing at Cape Poúlaris from afar, we quickly forgot what we had to go through until we entered the harbour. This bad weather, according to the weather reports, is only in the southern Aegean and the Cretan Sea.

22nd. Still waiting.

23rd. Still waiting for a northerly wind.

24th. We reefed sail but didn't leave. Too much wind. Northwesterly, like in the song about Nerantzoúla (when a text loses interest, like this journal during these days, it doesn't mean to say that life loses interest too). Shortly before midday we set out with the sails reefed, for Tílos (Piscopí on the map). In the evening we anchored at Éristo, at this hour truly panoramic. The bay, two miles in, faces south. We went to sleep tossed and rolled about by a terrible swell.

25th June. Yesterday, shortly before arriving, there appeared in the distance 'the crest of Nísyros' as Sikelianós* says in one of his poems. My way of looking at the world resembles above all the way in which poets look at it — they take part in it, they become part of it, they *are* the world, so to speak — *sunt* — rather than opposing it to themselves or making it an object.

We walked among the gardens as far as Megálo Chorió. It was the first day that I felt the heat of summer and the cicadas were singing: like fermenting grape-must. We went back to the boat. Sailed eastwards. We passed close to Cape Kefálas:

> *The cape — and on the hostile slopes*
> *The lone pine trees are bent to the ground,*
> *As though eternally dragging the boat of the north wind.*

Late in the afternoon we anchored at Livádi, and had a swim. We went to the monastery of St Panteleímon, dating (it says) from the 14th century, and restored in the 17th. Its feast day is the 27th July. Above the gate of the monastery is a Byzantine tower. The landscape seems to have come down from heaven for you to walk over it. And below, as far as the eye can see, is the sea, opening like a great gulf towards the south-west. Rocks, parched land, fearful precipices. There is a tradition that a great cypress tree at the monastery came from the Black Sea. Mountain water, plane trees, walnut trees: as a local song has it:

The cypress tree that grows so tall it overtops the tower,
And walnut trees whose leafy branches cover up the sun.

When we got back to Meghálo Chorió we saw a young mother
— both sad and smiling, a beauty with golden-brown hair —
who was holding her tiny baby, still unchurched, in a sling
— holding it, that is, tied in a strip of cloth that passed below
her armpit leaving her left shoulder and arm outside a
snow-white embroidered cloth that fell down almost to her
feet, while the baby was tucked inside — an old custom of indescribable charm. If you lifted the cloth slightly the little
thing gazed at you from within. I have only seen women in
Africa holding their babies so proudly and with such dignity.
The mother was slender as a reed, like the tall Black Sea cypress at the monastery which reared itself two or three times
higher than its brothers, in order to find the sun among those
shadowed cliffs — slender and youthful, almost a child, but
with the uncompromising, piercing glance of a she-eagle with
young. This girl carrying her child summed up the entire island, the gardens, the fruit trees (very few!), the herbs on the
hillside, the animals, the sky, the sea, all were concentrated in
the smiling human being who was re-enacting, eternalized in
her baby — 'for the millionth time', as the Irish poet says —
the ancient creative game of life.

Fare well, barren earth!

26th. We left for Nísyros, an island I would describe as lacking a harbour. We anchored at Pálous and went to Mandráki
at Emborió, to the crater of the volcano and to the village of
Nikiá which is as though suspended in the air, with its com-
munal square (a crescent of stone with low seats). As on Tílos,
there are little partridges feeding everywhere at this time of
the year, which are left unhunted. The island has not a drop

of water, apart from the rain-water that collects in the cisterns. Hot springs. No one had told me that Nísyros is covered in oak trees, whole forests of them.

27th. We left in the morning for Kálymnos, leaving the currents of Cape Kefálas on Kos on our right (a different Kefálas from the one on Tílos). A strong north-westerly wind is blowing and we get soaked: the weather is rough, the boat throws wave against wave in its passage, big swift waves. Yet

> *The summer sparkles everywhere*
> *Sun, sea and land all sparkle*
> *And only the pure-hearted and courageous man,*
> *One hand on the rudder and one on the sail*
> *Can comprehend the swiftness of the gods.*

To be pure amidst the radiance of life! That is what counts. The other things come later. And courage is never lacking.

At noon we anchored far out at Vlichádia, a small bay with a chapel dedicated to St Siderís. At Póthia, the harbour of Kálymnos, you can't find a space to tie up. We swam and rested.

In the afternoon, even though it's June, a violent local wind dragged our anchor and we were saved from going on the rocks with a great deal of trouble at the last minute by local fishermen. (This is apparently a regular occurrence in Vlichádia.) We tied up to the shore with a stout cable and escaped further injury. Something has gone wrong with the electrics of the boat and the starter isn't working. The crank handle doesn't do anything. The skipper has gone to find an electrician at Póthia, and I wait alone for a possible drop in the wind. I thought of the friend I am with, and of our mishaps, and wait for him to return. Meanwhile, Kálvos's dictum is again confirmed, as it was a few days ago:

I hear the mad raging
Of the wind.

From my brief experience today, after this afternoon's adventure, I have realized that the Kalymniots are terrific seamen.

28th. An electrician came today from Póthia and fixed the engine trouble. (The violent south-westerly wind lasted all night till 3 o'clock, made an attempt to start up again at 6, but now seems to be dying down — I see that I am writing on a page without a date, so I must be talking about yesterday.) We took a walk to Póthia. That evening we had dinner at Vlichádia. Now and again during the night, in the stillness of the riverbed you could hear the sweet tinkling of the sheep-bells, and at dawn the shepherd's whistle. The following day, feast-day of the saints Peter and Paul, we left.

It's the nameday of my only daughter. I think of her gentle, fine-tuned nature. I think of today's youth, and its banner-waving. In this century of world wars and social revolutions, when most people are blinded — or as they would say 'enlightened' — in running after an idea, become fanatical, hate each other, and finally turn mercilessly on their own fellows amidst the general slaughter, the best I can wish her for tomorrow — the very best — is to repeat within myself on her behalf two lines from W. B. Yeats's 'A Prayer for my Daughter':

An intellectual hatred is the worst,
So let her think opinions are accursed.

29th. We sailed all around the island starting from its east side, on our way towards Léros. Summer weather. Before leaving the island we went briefly to Vathí, with its long narrow harbour encircled by rocks — *ἐν λιμένι γλαφυρῷ*, the 'sheltered cove' of the Odyssey — and its sought-after early-season tangerines, which ripen at the beginning of November. We anchored off Xerókambos on Léros. In the afternoon we went to Lakkí at Plátanos, and walked. We spent one night at Xerókambos, anchored far out.

30th. Set out for Parthéni. Moored. Walked as far as Blefoúti. Lunch on the boat. Set off for Lipsí. Stopped for a little at the church dedicated to the Virgin Mary of Death (which was the name of the man who built it) and anchored in the little harbour of Lipsí, between the two churches of St Nicholas. We tied up to the buoy of a fishing boat. The harbour is protected, the only wind that it gets, and that only rarely, is from the south-west. (They call this wind *proveza* here, from the Venetian *provenza*.)

Today is the new moon. This afternoon at the Virgin of Death, the day (not the date — in the Aegean there are no dates, and you can be catapulted within minutes from summer into winter), the hour and the moment were one of those occasions when land, sky and sea are balanced in a threefold commonality whose central element is the light, which irradiates everything until the sun sets:

> *Hands of light, and feet of light,*
> *And all around you there is light*

as Solomós was the first to describe it in yet another of his sublime phrases. What is more, he had the courage to relate it to the other light which proceeds — or not, as the case may be — from within us:

> *Ah, the light which now adorns you*
> *Does not emanate from earth.*

Gradually the shadows start to close in. The new moon emerges as though seen through white cambric, and soon disappears, having turned to gold. Here again there exist the two original cells of which I spoke, farmers and fisherfolk. Everywhere there are animals grazing and terraces or steps of earth, golden-yellow from the harvested grain. Scattered around on the nearby hills and over all the cultivated amphitheatre are an incredible number of churches. Everywhere you go in Greece, whether it be the hills and valleys or the three-quarters of the country that is washed by the sea, you encounter the fathomless depth of the Orthodox faith with its 'houses of God', the faith which has always served the people as the basis for their spiritual truth: 'that thou mayest know how thou oughtest to behave thyself in the house of God, which is the church of the living God, the pillar and ground of the truth', as the Apostle Paul wrote to Timothy. Faith and language, farmer and fisherman or seaman, the two initial and enduring cells, bonded crosswise together like the lion, the angel, the calf and the eagle on the binding of the Four Gospels, or like the four primary elements, Thales' 'well-known four': in life and in death, the inexhaustible springs of ever-flowing water of a people who are the guardians of one of the most marvellous religions and languages in the world.

First day of July. (And yet, the fact of writing or noting down all these things in here deprives them of that irreplaceable savour of life, so different from the savour of writing. This problem has troubled me for years. Often in my life I've stopped writing, and a few times I have even stopped living in order to write. But how can it be otherwise? There are times, even, when writing saves life from disappearing. In the final analysis it is man who makes both his life and his writing either valuable or worthless. So from this standpoint, and from this standpoint alone, even writing may ultimately be legitimate for certain people.) We anchored in the late morning off Moscháto near Lipsí, intending to go on to Archioús in the afternoon. When we got there we anchored at Agoús, and tied up to the land with a cable as well. I have never seen a poorer place (and I've seen a lot of poor places in this country). I hope we will stay here for a little.

2nd July. I walked by myself to Alóna and then on to Glýpapa with its two anchorages in the shape of an E. Rocks and stones. No sand, but the water is clear once you get away from the awful seaweedy-marshy beaches of Agoús and Glýpapa. The wind has been blowing non-stop since 3 o'clock this morning. In the afternoon we left for Pátmos with the sails reefed. Squalls and waves; we arrived half-drenched at around sunset at the island, the great spiritual root of Christianity, and moored at Gríkos.

3rd July, Saturday. We rested; it's windy weather. It's blowing a gale at the big beach called Psilí Ámmos, where we had planned to go today. The sea is boiling up around Tsikniás. We're better off where we are.

4th July, Sunday. Being here on Pátmos and hearing today about the killings that are taking place in relation to the hijacking of the French airplane — Jews and Palestinians: an eye for an eye and a tooth for a tooth — makes me reflect that we persist in remaining focused on the Mosaic law, and that however much various thinkers dream and talk about a post-Christian era (as though man had attained to a Christian era and has now gone beyond it, or as though we were all obliged to agree with the blundering, unthought-out and unscholarly historical attitude which believes that because something has happened in historical terms, it has been left behind in real terms), we shall always remain pre-Christian, BC, far from the love and the Word of John the Evangelist, that pole star on the impenetrably dark horizon of present-day humanity.

In the morning we went to Lámbi, in the afternoon we went swimming at Melóï together with some foreign friends of mine whom I met up with here. Tomorrow we plan to return, God (or weather) permitting.

5th. Return journey. We leave Ikariá on our right — ominous Cape Pápas with its heavy seas (sailors will know what I'm talking about) — we pass Tsikniás and later Mýkonos and Délos, and drop anchor at night at Fínika on Sýros. We did 90 miles today. Wind still from the north-west. I had put my alarm clock safely in a locker, but the boat rocked so much that it took me ages to find it. We were pretty exhausted. Reefed sails. Sailing and motor sailing. Big seas. I was born into this ancient language and all day today I have been hearing the word *thalassa*, a Greek word without an etymology, beating against us fore and aft, its meaning and its name practically identical; and it was the first time that a word in common use suddenly took on a life for me to such a degree, and acquired so to speak such a quality of finality — and I can understand the irresistible magnetism of this language for all those who learn it in its first dazzling form, as it was at the time of Homer, to the point where they can say, as did Robert Fitzgerald in one of his letters: 'The sea ... likes to be called *thalassa* and *pontos* better than the wretched word "Sea", I am sure' (*Letters II*, 49).

6th July, Tuesday. We left Sýros with a dead calm (at last) and planned, leaving Yioúra [Yáros] on our right, to pass to the north of Cape Kéfalo at Thermiá and then enter the straits of

Tziá [Kea]. But ... whether in the carelessness of returning, or because of the drowsiness induced by the calm, we didn't stay on course and found ourselves north of Tziá (thereby going out of our way by some ten miles), and learnt that the sea does not forgive those who think they know her — without respecting her — or those who don't realize that on all the bridges and at all the rudders of all the boats in the world, those of them at least that sail according to the law of the sea and not of the land, there must be someone with their eyes open, to keep unerring watch by night and day.

FOURTH NOTEBOOK 1978

Friday, 9th June. I went down to Piraeus — writing this, I was stopped in my tracks (I don't know why, someone else can work that out), by the memory of the opening phrase of Plato's *Republic*: 'I went down yesterday to the Piraeus...' (God, what a country this is, where along with the sky and the climate, such precedents leap out at you without warning...) — anyway, I went down to Piraeus, and sailed with the ship of the line to Sýros, Páros, Náxos and so on.

10th June. Donoússa, Aiyáli, Katápola, Koufoníssia, Schinoússa... At Schinoússa I met up with the boat and the skipper, and the next day,

Sunday 11th June, we tied up at Stavrós on Donoússa, where to my great delight I met for the second time Father Damianós, the tiny parish priest of the island who comes from Amorgós, where he had been a monk (since childhood) at the Chozoviótissa monastery, and who welcomed us with the smile of a spiritual father, the kind of smile which reaches the eyes out of unutterable 'inner wealth', as Solomós put it, and with the hesychastic monk's serenity of heart. I spent the afternoon at Kéndro, and was reminded of Mersíni, Mesariá and Kalotarítissa. The next day,

12th June, at Kéndro, went swimming. They say that this year there hasn't been any calm weather; all through April and May there were storms and squalls. Now there are light north winds. In July and August the *meltémi* will start blowing. There are very few intervals.

13th June. We set off in the morning for Amorgós. The weather was of a clarity typical of the Aegean Sea, this place to which man has been linked for thousands of years, which he has inhabited, whose civilization he has guessed at (and sometimes found), leaving his traces or (as my friend Níkos Gátsos* writes in another work entitled *Amorgós*, in both jest and earnest) 'manifold examples worthy of his immortal descent' — until the technocrats of today invented ways to 'exploit' it, 'develop' it, 'make it profitable', and finally defile it — it is to be hoped only temporarily, or at any rate not irreversibly.

They are threshing and winnowing the grain. As we move away, looking at the mountains, the light settles on the bright yellow fields and does not move from there, as though it were being stored in them in order later on to nourish the few hours when there is no sun. The here blends with the yonder, land with sea, sky with earth. Everywhere the sacred union.

We reached Katápola at noon:

Dear fountain of Katápola, beloved crystal water,
Give my little bird a drink when it comes thirsting to you —

so runs the infinitely tender folksong, sprung from the ever-gentle folk sensibility. And it ends with a greeting to the midday offshore wind:

Katápola breeze
Blowing at midday.

We went up to the village of Amorgós by car and from there on foot to the Chozoviótissa monastery, where I find my previous visit recorded in the monastery guestbook: 17.8.1967. Ten years and more ago. They've repaired the way up now, extended the terrace over the terrifying cliff and installed an alarm system to inform Amorgós immediately in case of theft or any other emergency.

In the afternoon we leave for the Koufoníssia, but we didn't anchor, we decided to go on to our mooring at Schinoússa, where we arrived at night, tired out by the journey and the sea.

14th June. We spent all day on Antikéri with its church dedicated to St George and the big house belonging to the Frenchman Joseph Lyonet. Swimming was impossible on Antikéri because of the jellyfish. That night on Schinoússa we ate fish for the first time and drank wine from Santorini.

15th June. We spent all day at Irakleiá. Swam off Livádi in the morning. We anchored later at St George and in the afternoon went up to the church of the Virgin, one and a half to two hours' leisurely walk. Morning, afternoon and evening, each lovelier than the other. This is the tranquil 'temperate weather' that we pray for in the Liturgy. The moon getting towards the full.

16th June, Friday. Kalandó (Náxos) and then Alykós. There I left the others, who were going on to Sífnos. I spent one night on Náxos, and the next day took the boat back to Piraeus. Looking at the distant Cape Kolónes [Cape Sounion] on the return journey, I jotted down the following notes.

The sky, earth and sea of Greece (or of other places, but at the moment we're talking about Greece) only allow you a limited number of things to believe, build, sketch, live or speak.

The smallest wrong movement and everything can fall into the abyss. Sometimes its inhabitants have known this and have believed, built, sketched, lived (and spoken) accordingly. At other times they have missed the mark and tried to do other things which neither the sky nor the earth nor the sea in this country allow you to do. Things that the country won't take, as they say. The tradition and the faith can't take them, and neither can the language. People made these mistakes and either failed or else were out in their reckoning. Our own time seems to fall into that category in most of the things it does here and now. We have ignored the limits on the things permitted by the spirit of the place — we have ignored what is allowed.

We don't even seem to have noticed this overstepping of the mark, nor that it is merely a small part or symptom of the more general malaise of the world today, which constitutes the contrast between contemporary civilization and all the civilizations of the past, as well as, dare I say it, those that are to come, always supposing that there will be others in the future (for there is a serious possibility that there won't be anything to come at all). I don't know, practically speaking, the various details of what needs to be done — that will be solved, it's not the most difficult question. We have enough clever people — we always will have — and we even have some geniuses in certain areas, who could study the best solutions to the problems which are continually arising: practical solutions for practical problems, technical solutions for technical problems. That's not difficult. What is difficult is for the general principles to come into being which will provide the guidance for these important people, who are so proud of their formal advantages, diplomas, titles, studies, actions, and who in the absence of these general principles have practically succeeded in rendering the country unrecognizable, instead of humbly allowing themselves to be instructed by it, as well as by what it has been through. Instead of persisting and insisting on education, they should bow their heads and receive some education themselves, from a people who under difficult circumstances kept the face of the country unchanged and who always remained faithful to its spirit. I will never tire of repeating this refrain, in all its variations, about the wisdom of the people and its crucial importance for all that is essential and entire — and whoever doesn't want to listen can close their ears. I believe that if we do not take account of these general principles, nothing of any worth can be consolidated in this country of ours. Things will go right only when the educated people realize that there is no conflict between the village or island and their own education — between the moral imperative of Donoússa, for example, and the Greek Chamber of Commerce — and that it is not necessary to destroy the village or island (along with all the civilization that it has preserved unchanged till now, from the language to the faith), but that they should submit to it, learn from it, follow it, and fruitfully or creatively use it to incarnate each new element, *le nouveau,* as Baudelaire refers to it in his poem about those who — he sums up — will forever be diving down

Au fond de l'Inconnu pour trouver du nouveau.

Most educated people, who are separated from the folk and from life, don't leave us much to hope for. Have they no love for their country? I just don't know what to say. Too much reading has addled their brains. It is with sorrow that I always recall the guileless love of some foreigners (for whatever it may be: the people, the monuments, the land) which has helped them understand certain simple things, formed as they also are by their longer exposure to contemporary civilization — it is irrelevant whether or not these people were famous — such as Jean Pio, writing out of sheer love for our language, 'à cause de mon amour de la langue grecque', in the preface to his book *Modern Greek Folk Tales,* Copenhagen 1879, on the 15th August of that year, about '...le riche trésor...que le bas peuple des pays grecs possède encore, mais que le progrès des lumières menace de faire disparaître d'un jour à l'autre'. For over a hundred years love has been hammering at the door of the deaf. Is that a long time or a short time? No one knows. We must not lose heart while we wait. As St Paul says in his letter to the Corinthians, 'Love suffereth long...'.

The little boat hooted as it entered the harbour. (This is the last line of the most important short essay written by a friend now dead, the poet George Seféris, who was wounded, wherever he went, by the contrariness of our country. This is how I too will end this notebook, adding for consolation that all countries have their contrariness.)

FIFTH NOTEBOOK 1979

Looking over the past notebooks, it must be remembered that they encompass only a narrow section of the whole 360° spectrum of the Greek horizon. Nevertheless, there is no reason why certain conclusions should not be applicable and valid in relation to the whole circumference simultaneously.

1st June. Friday: we left Glifáda at 10.30 and used the motor almost all the time till evening, when we dropped anchor at Sérifos. There was a swell on the sea, it was stuffy and overcast. After so many months, I was unsteady on my feet until I rediscovered the rhythm of the sea and found my sea-legs, as the English expression so aptly has it. And there were one or two personal matters too: before embarking, my stomach was already upset by anxiety and by the stress of work undertaken during the last two months, when I was writing to a deadline (that spring I finished my essay, 'The Meaning of Literary Criticism', which had been commissioned by the journal *Ekivólos*).

2nd June. We spent the day on Sérifos. We swam at Livadáki, on the beach of coarse sand below St George. The church of St George, which stands in the little cemetery, is all curves and straight lines, clothed in layer upon layer of limewash which has been applied every so often, for years upon years, the limewash which is both natural and supernatural, used both for the health of the islands and for the other kind of

health. Limewash and wind are the two lords of these islands. And I will say something that relates to me personally,
though it also relates to every man and woman alive. At my
time of life (which is now considerably advanced) and in
the difficult times in which we live, I thank God that he still
permits me to savour his beauties with bodily, and his wisdom with intellectual, health, far from that final step over
which I was destined one day suddenly to stumble and fall —
I am writing this at a later date — ending up on the operat-
ing table in a hospital, writhing in pain and feeling that I was
at the end of my strength. There is a moment of total alone-
ness which every one of God's creatures will experience,
when some day, for whatever reason, its strength begins to
fail. This is the moment summed up (as always) by Cavafy
when he says:

in times of trial or when you near your end.

It is terrible to give yourself up *ut cadaver* into the hands of
others, incapable, burdensome, unprotected, a dead weight
with the prospect ahead of a death certificate, but also and
more generally with a sense that you are leaving the side of
those who are going upwards — I'm not talking here about
age — and crossing over to the side of those who are sur-
rendering, going downwards, who see the light fading. But
it is essential at this point not to forget the example from
the inexhaustible heritage of this country, in this case Plato's
Phaedo, which tells us that 'true philosophers make dying
their profession, and . . . to them of all men death is the least
alarming'. Some words about old age from the ancient tragedians, and a bullfight I once watched in San Sebastián, came
suddenly before me from far away at that moment. I gazed
at the event from the position I was in as the anaesthetist

was saying to me (the last thing I heard): 'You'll go to sleep now, good luck'. I faltered:

> *The strength that diminishes,*
> *Whether it flows like blood in the arena*
> *Of the animal which did not barter its vigour*
> *And is brought out dead amid the hurrahs*
> *Or else bends the knee to necessity*
> *And old age, or to the mighty illness*
> *That strikes you down suddenly.*

3rd June, Sunday. I walked to Tsilipáki and on the way back had a swim in a little bay. Tsilipáki is nothing to speak of, a swamp really, but you can moor there and be safe from the northerly winds. It's been blowing since yesterday: could it be the *meltémi*? June (but according to the old calendar it used to be May) is a bit late. In the afternoon I went up to Chóra and returned through the vegetable plots of Livádi, laid out in squares bordered with canes which protect them from the winds and hide them from the eyes of passers-by, real paradises of fruit, vegetables and citrus (lemon and orange trees). In the middle of the plain a stream comes down which in winter occasionally overflows its banks. They are now building an unnecessarily ostentatious and costly cement bridge, undoubtedly with the help of some politician who will not have to foot any of the bill, thanks to the scourge of the so-called 'credit by instalments' system which has filled the whole country with the ugliness of unfinished or halted works.

4th and 5th June. Waiting for the wind to drop. The weather forecasts are always worse than what is actually happening ('gale in southern Aegean' etc). Obviously, at this time of year there will be fine weather within the next few days. The boat from Piraeus calls in again on Wednesday the 6th.

On Tuesday afternoon we went to the monastery dedicated to the Archangels Michael and Gabriel. It's an old monastery, a monastery-castle really, in a beautiful position with a view over Serfopoúla and Pipéri. On the lintel of the church door I read the following inscription carved into the marble: 'I am God's general I hold the spear extended on high in the fear of God. I swiftly inflict retribution on all unbelievers. I am an angel of the heavenly battalion.' And in the centre is carved the date: 1447, Xenophón Pérgamos. From the monk I bought some wine made from a type of grape that is called *potamísio* [meaning 'of the river']: a strong, coarse wine, unadulterated. I also saw the date of the monastery's restoration: 1659. Apparently the monastery possesses some parchments with writing on them; these must certainly be known to Línos Polítis, whose love for the religion of his fathers and for palaeography takes him round all the monasteries in Greece. (Writing in 1983, I record the death of Línos Polítis in 1982.)

On the summit of Vódi there is a white mark that from a distance looks like a building, but which they told me is a white mineral outcrop which is locally known as *áxanos*. A curious name.

6th June, Wednesday. After starting to drop, the wind has started up again. In the afternoon we went on a short walk to Karávi, the second beach after Livadáki. The weather looks like calming down. We will probably leave tomorrow. Forecast and reality, foreknowledge and knowledge, are never identical.

The fact that we tacked to Sérifos has made me think of Danaë who escaped here from the storm in the carved chest with her precious baby son Perseus; the little innocent was asleep in her arms with just his lovely face visible, as Simonides writes, and heard nothing of the raging of the sea in the night as it towered up over their heads. The sight of his innocence helped the woman in her trouble. I also recall the lines from Shakespeare's *Tempest*, when Prospero miraculously escaped to the island in the rotten boat in which they had put him to sea to drown along with his beloved baby daughter Miranda — and again, she smiled and he took courage from her heaven-sent innocence in the midst of the raging storm.

Miranda: *Alack, what trouble*
Was I then to you!
Prospero: *O, a cherubin*
Thou wast, that did preserve me! Thou didst smile
Infused with a fortitude from heaven.

Two parallel lines which are not lost in infinity, but meet there.

7th, Thursday. We leave Sérifos. The church of St George accompanies us with its few dead, indicated by marble crosses which descend the slope of the little cemetery down as far as the sea. It is one of those Apollonian days that you get in the Aegean, with all the glory of sky and sea, all the abundance of the sun, a landmark June day. I am grateful for life and for death, the death for which life is steadily preparing, day in day out, with the busyness and patience of the bees. Today is a radiant sea libation for those in the shadow and darkness of death. Incarnation and apotheosis side by side, treading the same path.

We go on towards Despotikó near Antíparos, where we drop anchor in the late afternoon. It's an enclosed place, a safe mooring in all weathers without exception. The hills around it have been swept clean by all these days of wind. Sky and sea are merely variations of each other. Golden fields stretch up to the crests of the hills and down to the beaches. I think of the measure which this place teaches to all who heed such measures nowadays or who heeded them in previous times. And sometimes I seriously wonder whether a little sunlit threshing-floor on an island in the Cyclades, where man has laboured, is not now and has not always been better for his soul and its progress *sub specie aeternitatis* than Kant's *Critique of Pure Reason* or the last historic calculation that energy is merely mass multiplied by the square of the speed of light ($E = mc^2$). I really do wonder, sometimes, about this...

Opposite our mooring, up on Despotikó, is the chapel of the Virgin Mary of February, whose feast-day is the 2nd of February but because of the wind and rain at that time of year is now celebrated on the Monday of the Holy Spirit (which falls on the 11th of June this year), and today people went by boat from Antíparos, both men and women, to clean and prepare it. In connection with the churches on Lipsí in the notebook of 1976, I spoke of the immeasurable depth of our belief, and having seen the church of the Virgin Mary of February on Despotikó, I will add at the end of this notebook a few more observations related to our travels in general, which may help us arrive at a more correct estimation of the whole series of disasters with which our country has paid and is paying for its fallacies or its other wilful, costly and unnecessary follies.

In the afternoon we went over for a while to Antíparos and walked as far as St George's where Maroussó Patéli was buried, a 14-year-old girl who drowned in the well when she got tangled up in the rope and was dragged down. Her brother Dimítris offered us home-made *tsikoudiá*[1] in his little hut.

---

[1] Pomace brandy.

There is great poverty but also great freedom from care in this sea-girt untroubled place. Maroussó's girlfriends, Katína and Maria Mariníki, have put in the crypt where the grave-lamp burns a printed poem consisting of 38 fifteen-syllable verses, among them the following:

> *Mother mine I beg you do not step outside the door,*
> *And oh do not go near the well, the water up to draw.*

The whole place is overshadowed by the black wing of the tragedy. And with the tale of Maroussó, on this Aegean sea-shore with the tiny whitewashed chapel of St George floating in the radiance of the day like a white spoonful of *vanillia*[1] in a glass of clear water, I reflect that the Modern Greek poetic equivalent of the lines about the drowned King of Neapolis:

> *Those are pearls that were his eyes*

is the lament:

> *Seaweed her bridal wreath,*
> *Shells are her dowry*

made by the man who, if he were here, could legitimately narrate the story of Maroussó's fall into the well, as he narrated the fall of Akrivoúla into the sea and so many other tragedies, so many of the world's 'tribulations and sufferings', in his incomparably magical and poetical writings.*

8th, Friday. Left for Náxos. Mostly sail, and a little motor. Anchored in the bay at 5.30 p.m. Stayed on Náxos all Saturday;

---

[1] A thick, sticky sugar-based sweet flavoured with mastic and vanilla.

fine weather. From Apóllonas, where we went by car, you could see the islands of Ikariá and, faintly, Foúrnoi. In the little museum at Apeíranthos were the latest important archaeological finds: carvings done on stone, in particular a huntsman with a stag and astronomical charts of the heavens. Age of the caveman — I hadn't seen anything like them in Greece before. On Tílos in 1976 I saw fossils of small elephants, but I don't know from what epoch they dated.

10/6, Sunday. We passed north of Náxos on our way to beautiful Donoússa (Stavrós), rock-hewn and solitary. We went first to our old friend Kalotarítissa, had a swim, and then on to Stavrós, where we arrived at 7 o'clock. The heiromonk from Amorgós, Father Damianós — a truly holy man — was still there. The teacher is leaving this year to go somewhere else, and the children only finished their exams today. We'll stay the night here, keeping an eye open in case a south-westerly wind gets up, in which case we'll have to leave at once. The moon is full, the weather calm. (How could one ever imagine such a night as this could exist, in the terrible winters when the south-west wind blows up a real storm, and, as a fisherman once described it to me, 'churns up the underworld'.) I am glad to see the slopes of Myrsíni again, with one mill still functioning, and of Messariá. I've been told that the water of Myrsíni comes from Ikariá.

11th Monday, Feast of the Holy Spirit. First summer day, with summer heat, a summer swim, and a summer afternoon sleep. We were at Kéndro till 3 p.m., with not a soul around apart from ourselves. From now on, as school is over, a few people will start coming to Donoússa — only a few, but enough to change the way the island looks for a few weeks. It is so lovely here that these notes — which I make in order to remind myself of certain themes that are crucial for mankind, whisperings of life and death — seem washed-out clumsy copies of a matchless art, distorted echoes of a natural voice. Will I ever string these notes together, I wonder, like living fish on the glittering rod of language?

Tuesday 12th. We left Donoússa early in the morning, and at midday literally crept into Amorgós (Katápola) in a very rough sea.

13/6. The weather is getting worse. At this time of year the straits of Amorgós can be terrible. It's a strange June. We are stranded at Katápola. Yesterday's crossing from Donoússa was reminiscent of other months, not this one. The great waves, just below their crests where the foam breaks, turn emerald-green for a moment and you can almost see through them, so transparently do they reflect the sky or its light. You can be sure then that the weather will be stormy. Today someone tried to set out in his caique but had to turn back. We stay here on Wednesday as well. But on Thursday,

14/6 the skipper decides not to wait any longer. We set out at 6 in the morning and pass the point at sunrise. The crossing to Antikéri is about 8 miles, and the north-west wind hits us as we go along with our sails reefed, without a jib, just the engine. In the middle of the channel we get the full force of the wind and some massive waves, we are tossed about a bit but as soon as we get in the lee of the mountains of Náxos it's like entering a different world, and finally we anchor off Antikéri in calm water, have breakfast and later go for a swim. What you would here call a refreshing breeze turns into a raging wind in the straits of Amorgós, churning up a wild sea, proving the truth of the verse by Solon:

By winds the sea is lashed to storm, but if it be
Unvexed, it is of all things most amenable.

The skipper was right in deciding to leave.

At about 6 in the afternoon we saw Schinoússa once again, with its golden fields laid out alongside each other, an island that persists in retaining its agricultural character. (This is in contrast to the inhabitants of the Koufoníssia, who after the war changed their way of life from agriculture to fishing, and who now, through their shortsighted use of dynamite, are enriching themselves by impoverishing or enfeebling their wealth.) Where we are now, the day has been transformed into the second Apollonian day of our trip — the first was last Thursday the 7th.

15th, Friday. In the morning we went opposite, to Livádi on Irakleiá, for a swim, intending to pick up at Aï-Yórgis (Alykós) on Náxos two friends of the skipper's who were arriving from Piraeus. At Livádi there was a cool breeze but with wafts of summer heat — at last. I would give all the mountains and peaks in the world, with all their charms and joys, for a piece of coastline and the sea-level. From deep within the pages of Xenophon comes the cry that has always rung in my ears, the ancient cry in the many voices of those who have inhabited this island-strewn country of ours: *Thálatta, thálatta!*

When we returned from Aï-Yórgis in the afternoon, crossing between Irakleiá and Náxos, the sea filled with dolphins — left, right, near, far, at our bow, behind us, beside us — and then they moved off, leaping towards Nió [Íos], in the gold of evening which could have been either sun or sea, earth or sky. They came like a greeting from unconquered life in all its miraculous power, the high point of our journey.

And so as not to entirely forget elementary learning in this paradise — but learning which is alive, the learning of Homer or Solomós, not the learning of university studies and libraries — it must have been on some such sun-drenched day that Homer envisaged the god's passing, in book 13 of the *Iliad*, and imagined Poseidon's chariot racing over the waters of the Aegean. 'No mistaking the gods', *Ἀρίγνωτοι δὲ θεοί περ.* He has him descend from the summit of Mount Fengári on Samothrace, and after taking three strides, he arrives with the fourth at his destination, his eternal palaces in the depths of the sea, at Aegae — which for Homer was not a city in Achagía or Euboea (Kárystos) nor an island, but something like Mount Olympus was for Zeus, and, as proved by the word Aegae, the mythical capital or secret heart of the Aegean Sea and the dwelling of the sea-god. (Do we not think of Atlantis in the same way, as the drowned centre of the Atlantic Ocean?)

And since we have spoken of three strides and a fourth, I can't resist drawing a comparison, before we go any further, between them and the level footfalls of the other goddess, Liberty, as Solomós describes her trampling the tyrants in the decisive verse with which he apostrophizes the divinity:

> *Your sword aloft you raise,*
> *Forward three steps you pace,*
> *Tall as a tower you grow,*
> *At the fourth step falls the blow.*

In the same way, Poseidon's fourth stride brings him to his goal at Aegae. There he makes ready his chariot, the horses with their golden manes, the golden whip, himself clad in golden armour, to start the race over the waves. And everywhere, says Homer, leaving their lairs, the dolphins, knowing well their lord, leap in sport. And the glad water opened a way before him, and the horses flew on and the bronze axle beneath the chariot was never wet, until he reached the ships of the Achaeans.

In that place, much further north than where we are sailing at the moment, between Ímbros and Ténedos, there is a vast cave in the untrodden depths of the sea, where Poseidon reined in his horses, unyoked them, gave them ambrosia, immortal fodder, to eat, and fixed unbreakable and unopenable golden hobbles round their legs so that they would remain where they stood until their master returned. Then he sets off for the Achaean camp.

The gold of evening that I referred to above, saying that you could not tell whether it emanated from sun or sea, earth or sky, perfectly explains the flood of gold in the brief quotation from Homer, where in the space of a few lines the words golden ($\chi\rho\dot{\upsilon}\sigma\epsilon\omicron\varsigma$) and gold ($\chi\rho\upsilon\sigma\dot{o}\varsigma$) occur five times. First and foremost, of course, the word denotes divinity — in all spiritual traditions in the world, gold has reference to the supernatural element — but in Homer's *Iliad* it most obviously corresponds to the act of voyaging in Greek waters; and likewise, on a day or at an hour such as this, you are inevitably reminded by the world of creation around you of the well-known words which we have already pondered, by the great master Solomós:

> *Hands of light and feet of light,*
> *And all around you there is light.*

Amidst this triumphant apotheosis of brilliant light, and the sea-going cetaceans of the *Iliad*, I have just remembered — in connection with elementary knowledge and its multi-lingual brotherhood — the sorrowful northern voice from Milton's *Lycidas,* pleading with the dolphins for the young man, Edward King, lost in the Irish Sea in August 1637:

And, O ye dolphins, waft the hapless youth...

In the evening at Aï-Yórgis, Irakleiá, we had white *nyktéri* wine from Santoríni and cheese from Náxos and locally-made wheaten bread at the eating-place run by the village president, whose surname was Kovaíos. I learned that he is the brother of Father Damianós of Donoússa, who spent 25 years in the Chozoviótissa monastery on Amorgós. In this way, along with the sea and the waves, the sky and the islands around, the fields and the fishing caiques, the people too are bound to each other by blood or by relationships that are never disproportionate to the general scale of the region, a scale which is wholly human, measured and designed always in terms of specific needs and practices, never in terms of theory and prejudiced or abstract planning.

We returned to Schinoússa by night.

16th, Saturday. Today, the last day before the return to-morrow — I shall be leaving with the ship of the line from Schinoússa — we set out in the morning under sail, and with a light wind we went to one of the Koufoníssia, the one that is uninhabited, swam and spent the afternoon there, and then went on to the other, the inhabited one, where on the little sandy beach of the Italian woman,[1] the round white well and two gulls side by side awaited us, who flew off as soon as we landed. Their footprints in the sand were like two double rows of little anchors, one after the other. Inland, towards the house of the Italian woman, with an incomparable view over Kéros, Glaroníssi and all the other islands and islets in this blessed

---

[1] This is what the islanders call a Greek woman (whose name they don't know), the daughter of a wealthy Greek from the north of the country, who was briefly married to an Italian and is now divorced, and who owns a big publishing concern in Rome.

archipelago south of Náxos, among the little slopes which descend from the house to the beach, near the lentisks and the scrub oaks, you can make out in detail the lightly drawn tracks of the adders which apparently come down to drink at the well. Snake-tracks mingled with the small ribbon-like trails of the lizards. We had observed these traces before, in other years, in the immaculate sand.

Today is one of the loveliest days we have had on this trip. There is utter peace. All the islands are floating, their outer rims suspended in air. With just an imperceptible change in the laws of nature, and with a corresponding attempt on our part to approach nearer (within ourselves) to that unapproachable 'O you of little faith, why did you doubt?', one could imagine today that it might even be possible to walk effortlessly upon the sea.

* * *

As promised, I will now add 'a few more observations' (I quote from the page written on Thursday 7th) 'related to our travels in general, and which may help us arrive at a more correct estimation of the whole series of disasters with which our country has paid and is paying for its fallacies or its other wilful, costly and unnecessary follies.' I was referring then to the churches at Lipsí and to the church of the Virgin of February at Despotikó, which was being decorated by the people of Antíparos for its feast-day, that had been moved from the 2nd February to the Feast of the Holy Spirit. The circuitous route that I am about to take may seem rather a long way round, but it is ultimately concerned with the country and closely connected with it.

Seeing our whitewashed chapels and being aware of the fact that whether you enter the Cathedral of St Sophia in Constantinople or St George's chapel at Antikéri, you are entering the same space, spiritually speaking, my thoughts turn to another Orthodox country, not small and poor but great and wealthy. I consider what I am about to say as common to all countries, and I believe that if you abandon your spiritual tradition, whatever it may be, then even if you gain the whole world, you are nothing. I am referring to certain recent upheavals in this country and to the wrong-headed thinking that is invariably costly and of which, alas, not all of us are aware. Young people today, in particular, are fatally ignorant with regard to the last fifty years of this century (I am writing this in 1980), and so-called 'unbiased' history does all it can to addle their brains even further. I set down the following measured thoughts — measured in the sense that they are few, not in the sense that I pride myself on possessing the 'right measure' — in the faint hope that they might be found useful. That is their main *raison d'être*. And in pursuit of this goal I will not use my own voice. For the great wealthy nation I am thinking of, as opposed to our own small poor one, I shall be using the voice of an eyewitness — the only voice that would have got a hearing there.

Young people today in Greece — I am speaking more about the young people in universities or a significant proportion of them, rather than about young people in general, who roam free, apparently, *extra muros* — are being pulled along by various different people, who are possibly well-intentioned but who are sadly irresponsible, if not indifferent in a deeper spiritual sense towards their country and its people. Young people, therefore, are being dragged into following Marx and Lenin — as during the last century certain Greeks were similarly dragged along in the footsteps of the Enlightenment or of Voltaire (with similarly blind reactions from the rest of the bigoted brigade) — and I fear that only with great difficulty will they be able to raise their heads above this towering, magnetic wave which presently engulfs them and look both at their own tradition (which they have left behind and don't even deign to look at) and also at Marx and Lenin, whom they see through distorting lenses which do double injustice to both, over-valuing or deifying them in some cases, and simultaneously under-estimating them in others. If these young people do not raise their heads above water now, I am afraid that they will remain intellectually isolated for the remainder of their entire life.

This is not the place to analyse spiritual tradition. Without it 'was not anything made that was made', as St John's Gospel puts it. All peoples and all individuals are aware of this, and it needs no further explanation. I spoke above about the 'responsibility towards [one's] country'. Again, this is not the occasion to analyse what we mean by 'country': we all know what it means. However, I also spoke of 'responsibility towards the people'. And in this connection we will have to make special mention of 'the people' and dwell a little longer on them. (We should really be standing before them and saluting.)

Since there clearly exist in Greece today certain factions, whether small or large is not our concern, who are given over wholeheartedly to foreign patrons (as in the last century, according to Makriyánnis, there were the 'Anglicisers' and the 'Frenchifiers' and the 'Russianisers', to wit: 'Dawkins wants us to be English, Rouen French, and Katakázis Russian; and there isn't a single Greek left', and 'I was always suspicious of people who throw in their lot with foreigners'), one wonders what there can possibly be in common between the Greek people as we know them and a people who for centuries were ruled and still are ruled by an all-powerful centralized authority, in a vast and wealthy country occupying one sixth of the earth's surface, where over 100 different languages are spoken, and whose population is estimated today at over 250,000,000. What can they have in common? always bearing in mind the fact that many things may exist in common between all peoples, and that for centuries the Russian people and ourselves have shared the spiritual heritage of Orthodoxy, to which the great Slavonic soul has made its own unique contributions, from the colours of Andrey Rublyov (1370–1430) and the writings of Abbakoum (c.1620–1682) to the classics of Russian literature. Nevertheless, what do our social and economic conditions have in common, that we should have imposed on us, in accordance with the dictates of the kind of people I mentioned at the beginning, the same sort of rulers and the same type of ruling system as they have? unless it be considered common ground between us that both they and we may once have read Marx's *Das Kapital* and become Marxists. Especially since their present regime has been sustained by force of arms — which is hateful to most people in this country — ever since Lenin's coup in November 1917. That coup rendered null and void the elections for a Constituent Assembly which had been fixed for November 25th and, of course, the Assembly itself which had been arranged for the 12th December 1917. The Russian Revolution of February–March 1917, which came as a shock to everyone (including Lenin himself who was in Switzerland) had decided all this. But Fate decreed otherwise. I don't know whether the various people I mentioned above draw the attention of their young followers to these points as much as they do to other points.

Let me state in advance my attitude to Marx's philosophy. As far as I am concerned, who am above all interested in the purely human aspect of philosophy, what is of ultimate importance is not to save man from capital but to save him from himself. (From then on, we are saved as a matter of course from capital and from everything else as well.) This is not the moment to examine Marx's philosophy or its political implications — all we can say here is that it is not Marx's fault if we use his thinking to annihilate people or to oppress entire nations. However, as regards Lenin's tactics, or rather his strategy (for his was a party with a military-style discipline, always ready to monopolize power by force of arms where circumstances permitted) which is so much admired by university students, it is worth pausing for a moment to look at it from the point of view, not of Lenin's party, but of the people — and at that time Maxim Gorky was, beyond any doubt, a true son of the people.

I don't know whether the people I referred to earlier permit the students in universities — i.e. the little children — occasionally to open the cupboard (of history) when they — i.e. the grown-ups — have gone out for a walk, or even whether they themselves are always keen to know what is in that cupboard, but I think that truth should not be hidden, whether or not we are aware that it is shut away somewhere. It is our job to knock and have the door opened, to seek and find, and not confine truth to the 'truth' that we personally prefer, and, worst of all, to defend this one-sided 'truth' of ours by means of the gun or, under different circumstances, through the Catholic Church's Index of Forbidden Books. I am speaking of those who drag the young along in their wake, but also and more generally of the politically aligned intelligentsia, right or left, to remind them that we underrate man, be he young or no longer young, when we do not allow him to judge for himself on all things, and it seems at best inconsistent, if not far worse, to want on the one hand to stop the 'exploitation of man by man' — or to stop supporting *katharévousa* and the looting of our patrimony — and on the other hand to belittle man by not setting him above ourselves, not just on paper or in theory (in the purely ornamental articles of some impeccable Constitution, for example) but in honest everyday fact. And by not allowing man to judge all things freely for himself, we belittle him at least as much as those who exploit him economically. We belittle him when we confine him intellectually, like animals herded into a pen.

Gorky — and here, for the last time, I question whether young people in universities and those whom they trail after know or even wish to know these things (I think the answer is no) — brought out a newspaper in 1917 which was called *New Life* (*Novaya Zhizn*). The first edition circulated in May (or according to the old calendar, in April) of that year. The newspaper was closed down by Lenin in July 1918. Lenin was in favour of the party, Gorky of the people, and after his paper was closed down he battled, as before, to save countless people from fragmentation, prison, illness, hunger and all the consequences of political terrorism. At this point one may agree with Chekhov's estimate that in the case of Gorky, it is the human individual rather than the man of letters who lives on. Maxim Gorky never became a party member, and he wrote the following in issue 6 of the newspaper *New Life* (8th May 1917):

'People who have become like wood and stone under the pressure of a faith professed by them have never won my sympathy. I can admire theoretically their strict consistency, but I cannot like them.

'I shall say more: I consider myself a heretic everywhere. In my political views one can probably find no small number of contradictions which I cannot and do not wish to reconcile, because I feel that for the harmony of my soul, for my spiritual tranquility and comfort, I should have to kill precisely that part of my soul which most passionately and painfully loves the living, sinning, and — forgive me — pitiful Russian man.'

We can understand that in politics, the only person who feels 'a heretic everywhere' is the man who retains free judgement, free not in relation to his opponents or his enemies — his 'class enemies' as Lenin would say — but in relation to his friends and his relatives (which is hardest of all), and that Lenin could not allow a heretic to produce his newspaper in freedom, once he realized that this heretic loved the people more than the party and considered no creed superior in importance to man, to 'the living Russian' who before his very eyes suffered the tortures of political terrorism, not theoretically and bodilessly and in the abstract, but in real life, in his flesh and his bones, during that terrible time.

The extreme difficulty of remaining free in one's judgement in relation to one's friends and relatives is clearly evident not only in the case of Lenin, but even more so in the case of Stalin, who later, with his macabre acts of 'cleansing', in the end left none of his friends and relatives uncleansed. When you put the party above the people or your creed above your fellow-man and you become the leader of that party and the depository of your creed, it is easy for you one day to say that you are both the party and the creed, to say once more: '*L'État, c'est moi*'. From then on it is downhill all the way. Each day sees this unpalatable truth verified in action.

In issue 177 of his paper (23rd November 1917), Gorky writes:

'Threatening with hunger and violence all who do not agree with the despotism of Lenin and Trotsky, these "leaders" justify the despotism of authority against which all the best forces of the country fought so painfully long.'. . .

(Shortly before, in issue 174, on the 20th November 1917, he had written: 'Does not Lenin's government, as the Romanov government did, seize and drag off to prison all those who think differently?')

'Lenin himself, of course, is a man of exceptional strength. For twenty-five years he stood in the front rank of those who fought for the triumph of socialism. He is one of the prominent and striking figures of international social democracy; a man of talent, he possesses all the qualities of a "leader" and also the lack of morality necessary for the role, as well as an utterly pitiless attitude, worthy of a nobleman, towards the lives of the popular masses.

'Lenin is a "leader" *and* a Russian nobleman, not without certain psychological traits of this extinct class, and therefore he considers himself justified in performing with the Russian people a cruel experiment which is doomed to failure beforehand.

'The people, worn out and impoverished by war, have already paid for the experiment with thousands of lives and will be compelled to pay with tens of thousands, and this will deprive the nation of its leadership for a long time to come.

'This inevitable tragedy does not disturb Lenin, the slave of dogma, or his cronies — his slaves. Life in all its complexity is unknown to Lenin, he does not know the popular masses, he has not lived with them; but he — from books — has learned how to raise these masses on their hind legs and how — easiest of all — to enrage their instincts. The working class is for a Lenin what ore is for a metalworker. Is it possible, under all present conditions, to mould a socialist state from this ore? Apparently it is impossible; however — why not try?'

A few days later, on December 8th 1917, the evening edition of *Pravda* contained the following statement, which from then on was to be the stereotyped answer of Leninists to all who did not agree with them: 'The writer who for so many years had the ear of the proletariat has gone over to the ranks of those who make it their main business to slander the working-class movement.' From that day to this, much ink has been spilled over things which, in my opinion, are very simple. Simple, because ultimately no one can conceal his intentions. And after all, in these cases, the ink merely leaves a stain. What is worse is that sometimes human blood also gets spilled.

Again, in issue 225 (30th January 1918) of *New Life* Gorky writes:

'A wholesale extermination of those who think differently is an old, tried method of the domestic policy of Russian governments. From Ivan the Terrible to Nicholas II this simple and convenient way of combating sedition was freely and widely used by all our political leaders; why, then, should Vladimir Lenin renounce such a simple method?

'And in fact he does not renounce it when he frankly declares that he will shrink from nothing to eradicate enemies.'

Gorky had no illusions about whom he was addressing. In issue 175 (21st November 1917) he writes:

'I am aware that the future of the people is of no concern to the impassioned dogmatists; for such rigid thinkers the people are merely the necessary material for their social experiments; they are untouched by the thoughts and feelings which break the heart of every true democrat. I am well aware of all this, yet I do not speak in order to be heard by these people.'

As we said, the newspaper was closed down and all Gorky's efforts to restore it to circulation came to nothing.

The extracts quoted above were written at a time when events were still unfolding. There are many dimensions to the issue. What concerns me is the purely human aspect. It is obvious that after so many years, with all the added perspective gained since then and 'as part of this return to the past', as Cavafy says, Gorky's conclusions have greater significance today and his message ought to be more closely listened to by the people to whom he was speaking in order to be heard

— if, that is, successive generations learn anything at all (through looking back), a point which I fear will remain forever debatable. I said that he ought to be heard. But I doubt whether, in spite of all our added perspective, his message is listened to more attentively. It is superfluous for me to add that all such remarks (and this is something that gets forgotten by the people I referred to initially and by all intellectuals in general) are made in the knowledge that only Russians can speak *authoritatively* about Russians and about what exactly did or does go on or what didn't or doesn't go on as regards the Russian people; the rest of us can, of course, talk about it, but we are as it were out of the game, ranged in chairs looking on. Our judgement is not the sound itself but an echo, as different as night and day. In particular, we cannot speak *authoritatively* about the purely human aspect — as we can talk about the Constitution, the dams, the schools, the dwellings, heavy industry, production, armaments or the budget (and even in these cases we run the risk of not always having information which is absolutely accurate).

Anyone wishing to know more about the Gorky–Lenin connection and who would like to open the closed cupboard, in relation to the problems which educated young people in this country (and not just in this country) always take so long to come to grips with, can find the answers in the following texts (and ultimately in himself):

1. Bertram D. Wolfe, *The Bridge and the Abyss. The Troubled Friendship of Maxim Gorki and V. I. Lenin* (New York, F. A. Praeger, 1967).

2. Maxim Gorky, *Untimely Thoughts, Essays on revolution, culture and the Bolsheviks 1917–1918* (Paul S. Eriksson, Inc., New York, 1968).

I said that the subject has many dimensions. I shall now quote from the book *La société française*, written in 1979 by

Cornelius Castoriades, whose knowledge of the political and historic dimensions of this subject is almost unparalleled and whom no one can seriously accuse (although everything is possible) of having 'gone over to the ranks of those who make it their main business to slander the working classes'. The following is what he says about Lenin, and it is also an oblique reference to the fate of Lenin's writings: 'Dans la cinquantaine de volumes des *Oeuvres complètes* de Lénine, une phrase au moins restera éternellement vraie: "En politique il n'y a que les imbéciles pour croire les autres sur parole"' (p. 260). This phrase is indicative both of the 'cynicism' of which Gorky spoke as being necessary for a 'leader', and of the political philosophy of Marxism-Leninism in general, which is no other than the eternal philosophy of politics, the philosophy of Caesar or of power in all its shameless nakedness, and which comes retrospectively to verify the tragic intellectual contradiction experienced by Maxim Gorky in his *Untimely Thoughts,* written in 1917–1918, from which I quoted a few extracts above. It is the world of grandiose history within which we live, the kingdom of Caesar, and Gorky, along with all those who were in thrall to the positivism of the 19th century and the unlimited capacity of science — along, that is, with Marx and Lenin — was convinced not that this world could get better or worse (which is always possible) but that it could change, and indeed that one day, from being the kingdom of Caesar it might turn into the kingdom of God.

If I have lingered for some considerable time on themes which bear no obvious relation to the things that I never tire of looking at from the deck of this boat, it may be forgiven, I believe, simply when one thinks of what this country has been through as a more or less direct result of these same themes, together with countless of our contemporaries (Achaeans or

Trojans), who have been 'abused, hounded, reviled' for years on end in the name of an illusory cause, a 'phantom' as Euripides says in his *Helen*, tasting so many poisons, experiencing unspeakable disappointments and disaster upon disaster, for a non-existent Helen, for a bit of cloud, until finally the best among them have asked: 'was it only for a cloud that we struggled so much?'

Now that we are on the subject of distant lands, having started with a reference to our own little chapels and seas, I cannot refrain from mentioning what I consider to be Gorky's crowning glory, an out-of-the-way glory, won far from the domain of the glory that is as it were general, or public or common. There is a little book by Maurice O'Sullivan, *Twenty Years A-Growing* (1933), with a prologue by E. M. Forster, the friend of Cavafy, in which he compares it for its freshness to the egg of a seabird laid this very morning. And the book does, in fact, describe the first twenty years in the life of a boy on the Blasket Islands, outside Dingle Bay, low down on the west coast of Ireland, pounded furiously and unceasingly by the great waves of the Atlantic Ocean, and where sometimes it is only the crying seabirds that can fly unharmed through the storms. It is a book of virgin purity, created out of life rather than art, whose only literary influence is Gorky's *My Childhood*, a copy of which had made its way, God knows how, to those islands, which at the start of the century still lived in the neolithic age (like Kalotarítissa on Donoússa), and was read by the writer, on whom it left a profound impression. The world in which this lucky book by Gorky made its appearance bears obvious similarities to ours, as these journals have attempted to describe it now and again, similarities which are also evident in another book written by another Irishman, the poet John Synge, first published in 1907, about the Aran Islands, north of the Blaskets, outside the gulf of Galway. I forgot to say that Maurice O'Sullivan and his wife and children later lived with villagers in Connemara, a little further north still, and in 1950 he was drowned while swimming in those dangerous waters. The similarities between the two countries are strong and the parallels evident. In Synge's *The Aran Islands* there is even an explicit reference to contemporary Greece ('as in modern Greece') when he refers to the fact that in many places here we give people names according to their different occupations, whereas there, where everyone has the same occupation, the distinction is made differently. During the very cold days of winter the children go to school each carrying a sod of turf for the fire, as in many of our own villages children carry a log. The same wild keening breaks out there at the spectacle of death as in our own Mani. 'These people', writes Synge, 'make no distinction between the natural and the supernatural.' The similarities between us are many, as are the differences, but when speaking of spiritual traditions and of a focus on things which belong to a different, mythical world of legend, one's mind involuntarily goes back to those places which teach people to 'make no distinction between the natural and the supernatural', and to communicate with each other in the ancient language of necessity, which is at the same time the language of truth and of poetry.

Thus, the circle or detour that we have made is ultimately, I believe, concerned with this country and closely connected with it.

* * *

A hot summer's day, totally still; late afternoon. We are returning to Schinoússa (so that I can take the boat tomorrow, Sunday), and as we approach the jetty from afar, tell me, reader, does any writing possess the capacity to fill your heart, as our hearts at this moment on the sea are filled, with the very essence of that first sudden breath of evening coolness being exhaled by the land as we draw near? Whatever art you employ, it can't be done, it isn't possible. Voice and writing, the spoken and the written word, do not create life, they create something which looks like life but isn't — as Plato said in the *Republic*: 'if [the craftsman] does not make that which really is, he could not be said to make real being but something that resembles real being but is not that.' Like a mirror, they do not produce 'the reality and the truth', but only 'the appearance of them', and we must not forget that the imitator, or, to speak more philosophically, the mimetic art, is 'three removes from the truth' (first comes God or the natural begetter and secondly the creator). As an imitator at the third remove, at the end of such a day of grace as this has been, and without any illusions that through writing I might be able to recreate life, I too now bring this notebook to an end.

SIXTH NOTEBOOK 1981

11th June, Thursday. We sailed all day. This year the boat is small, about six metres; when you go below you have either to stoop or else sit down, and at night there is only just sleeping room for me and the skipper, but there are various conveniences regarding the sails and you have the advantage of being able to moor practically anywhere, however shallow the water. We stopped now and then to take a swim. We tested certain details — it was the boat's first trip — checked her over, suggested changes, made sure of some things. At Dokós we spent a peaceful night, by ourselves. There was a sense of returning to the world of God, defined by the earth and the firmament above, and of separation from the world of man as it is defined today; two worlds (for people nowadays), one world (for all other civilizations).

Recently I have been going over in my mind certain things common to us all, to any man and any woman, in the chronicle of men and women, who each time seem to say to each other (dazzled mutually by their love):

> *The taste that I had taken of this world*
> *now has the added flavour of your beauty.*

It is as though each man and each woman were saying it to each woman and each man.

12th and 13th, Kiparíssi, Kavomaliá, Vátika.

14th, Sunday. This morning there was a north wind blowing, and we went across to Elafónissos. Previously it was the sails that were the reality on all seas, now it is the motor. When the sails were the reality they functioned properly. Now, even when they function properly (as in sailing) — what with all the improvements in sail design as a result of the new mathematics, in conjunction with the new synthetic fabrics, in the years after the war — they are no longer the reality itself, but its heritage.

15th, Monday, Feast of the Holy Spirit, Patron of Vátika, where they celebrate today. On Elafónissos there are long sandy beaches at Nissiá tis Panayiás and Símos. We are moored in a real fishing port, with a proper fleet of fishing boats. The people are different from the people of the Moréa. The old men say that they came here and settled the island as refugees, after the fall of Crete, when a lot of Cretans went to the Ionian Islands. They bear more resemblance to Cretans than to the inhabitants of Vátika opposite.

16th, Tuesday. Nissiá tis Panayiás. A long sandy beach stretching all the length of the bay, which reminds me of the melancholy Breton poet and author of *Les amours jaunes*, Tristan Corbière:

> *Bénite est l'infertile plage*
> *Où, comme la mer, tout est nu…*

I murmur to myself:

> *Blessed is the barren shore*
> *Where, like the sea, all is naked…*

'Ah, if only you were with me,' says the man to the woman and the woman to the man, 'here and now, you who are absent. Aren't you perhaps saying the same thing? Wishing I were there beside you?' Then they do what the large and small hands of the clock do, they meet. Each time 'this' happens in the life of two people, the clock strikes the hour. What hour did it strike at this or that coming together? And what is this irresistible desire to be continually and with such rapture at each other's side? I just don't know the answer — I swear it on the tiller under my hand, as I sail over these seas!

Blessed is the barren shore.

And blessed also, ten times over, is this love that dazzles two people.

17th, Wednesday. At the first gust of wind, as we were moored close to the rocks in deep water and were afraid we might be thrown against them, we left during the night (3.30 on Wednesday morning) from Nissiá tis Panayiás and arrived when dawn was in the sky at Símos with its two sandy beaches. We dropped anchor, tired out. The skipper lay down for a bit. I went by myself to the second sandy beach, thinking about 'this'. There was an onshore wind. I cooled off gratefully in the dawn sea. It seemed to me then that somewhere nearby a man was speaking to a woman who was waiting for him:

> *In places where sleeping mermaids had walked*
> *I chose and gathered and brought before you*
> *All the riches of night and all the ornaments of day*
> *Little feathers, twigs of foam, the best of everything,*
> *Shells, fish scales, pebbles, transparent shellfish*

Like half-closed eyelids: so that yours would open
And you would ask them to tell you what the spells are
that bind us.

On the sea-bottom, in ripples, the sand is a reflection of the ripples of the fair-weather clouds in the sky, both of them finely drawn, immaculate, up high and down below. Sky and earth are one. In Heraclitus' words, 'Hades and Dionysius'. Life and death. Once again,

Blessed is the barren shore.

We hoisted the sail and went across to Tsirígo [Kíthyra].

* * *

Before we left, and while I was swimming, my ears filled with the voices of birds, waves, the wind, the breathing of heaven and earth, all harmonizing in a mysterious and seductive song, I remembered another song, a human song this time, with its own human features, which I once heard — again in summer, in the month of August — being sung without the words, just the tune, with the sweetness of a tired old voice which quavers and wobbles like the person. The wood of that voice was cracked and broken, yet it possessed an imponderability — how shall I put it — that inexplicable quality with which things are gradually overlaid by time, through cultivation (in the agricultural sense), through the various events that happen, and through the wisdom that accumulates as time flows on.

I was lying at the time in a hospital bed, gravely ill, and through the open window which looked onto the porch, which was where all the patients who could get up either sat or shuffled around, there was visible (I can see it before me now) first a weeping willow tree, then some light-green pine trees, then some dark-green pine trees, the outline of Mount Hymettus, and the sky. As soon as the tune without words began to come softly from the lips of the singer, it was as though the place was transformed into a river-bank, where a river, unheard and unseen, followed the cadences of the voice, greening over the dry Attic earth, permeating everything with its coolness.

Just as when sometimes there passes before us a very beautiful woman, extraordinarily beautiful I mean, far and away more beautiful than other women, uniquely so, arousing within us, perhaps, the memory of something read long ago, the amazed question of the Chorus in Milton's dramatic poem *Samson Agonistes* when Delilah passes by:

But who is this, what thing of sea or land?

— so at that moment, lying on a hospital mattress, I wondered, fascinated, what this song might be that came from a world of myth and legend? With its beautifully crafted harmony, rooted deep in the tradition of demotic music, its melodic line recounted, with steadfast endurance, unbearable sufferings, returning over and over again to its simple and sorrowful theme. It spoke (I asked for the words later) about the destiny that loomed over us from the start of the revolution of 1821, when Braïmis burnt the whole of the Morea and, as is always the case with fires, not only the people were lost but also the birds in the sky and the animals on the earth. We know that during that period Theodore Kolokotrónis* used to go off every so often to the Ionian Islands. I am not going give a description of the melody, as Milton describes Delilah in his poem, but I will just say this. The song begins in spring, in April or May, and the first distich is a simple statement of total catastrophe and despair. Even the voices of spring are absent. The distich is the introduction to an epitaph. It breaks off suddenly and leaves us on the borders of some lost world. The song continues, of course, and the three remaining lines are a foretelling of the hard destiny that was to be ours in the course of time, a hard destiny for so small a country, and we are given a brief glimpse of valour (which we so sorely lack) and also of enviable strength in the face of unrelenting circumstances and blighted times. This is what the inconsolably bitter song had to say:

> *On all the mountains where I walked and all the little*
> > *hillsides*
> *In March and April of this year I heard no cuckoo calling.*
>
> *Thódoras heard it where he stood on Zákynthos's castle*
> *He puts his spyglass to his eye to see what it can show him*
> *He sees how ample is the sea, how narrow the Moréa.*

I don't know why, but I was reminded of this song, while I was swimming, by the dawn chorus of the birds, the breeze and the waves breaking in foam on the second of the two magical sandy beaches at Símos.

Ours is a narrow country, in the middle of a wide sea.

* * *

18th and 19th. A strong westerly wind is keeping us tied up here at Ayía Pelayía. At midday on Friday the 19th we went to Diakófti, which is the only secure anchorage in the whole of Tsirígo because it is cut off to the north by the island of Makroníssi. I once spent a summer here, in Diakófti, with my daughter in one of the wonderful houses with very thick walls and arched roofs, warm in winter and cool in summer, with a separate cooking area and wide stone seats in the main room where one can lay out one's bedding and sleep. Almost no one has arrived yet on holiday. We are completely alone.

I have been reflecting that there are three roads that a man can take in confronting the universe. All three roads together, and each one of them separately, presuppose a different approach. There is no opposition between them, nor are they contradictory, there are simply differences. It is man who creates the oppositions and contradictions. But it is also man who creates the patterns by means of which we confront the universe, and as we said in another notebook, each of us creates his own patterns

The first road is the road of faith, in the absence of which neither of the other two roads would have any existence, for no matter which road you follow, inasmuch as you continue to live, it means that you have accepted life, and that since you accept it (whether consciously or unconsciously) you do not only believe in it but you fight, as long as you have it, to keep it from being taken from you, or continually to improve it insofar as you can, whether it is your own life that is in question or the lives of others, sometimes of all others. Faith, in other words, is our life inasmuch as we accept it, it is that which we (consciously or unconsciously) accept and in which 'we live and move and have our being', as long as we have 'the promise of God in our bodies' and are 'alive' as Makriyánnis says; faith, in the words of St Paul, is that which is 'not far from every one of us', or, in the vivid imagery of the Koran, closer to man 'than the vein in his neck'. The road followed by faith in confronting the universe — for those who consciously accept that this is our common road — goes according to the introductory words of Genesis: 'In the beginning God created the heaven and the earth', which says it all, once and for all, uncompromisingly, and on the basis of this statement man orientates his entire life (and all it contains) from cradle to grave, focusing more on inward beauty — 'grant that I may become fair within', taught Socrates in the *Phaedrus* — or as Solomós called it 'the wealth within', in the realization that even if he learns all secrets and all knowledge he can never get anywhere without love, and will be left in the end naked and a danger to other men. For almost two thousand years our people have followed this spiritual tradition, insofar as human beings are able, with their human capacities, to follow a difficult road which begins with the fall and ends in sanctity. If in the language of politics or sociology the people are now sovereign (and if this is not merely playing with words), then what man is so superior to the people as to venture to change their beliefs? And whence will he derive the right to decide what other men should believe?

The second road one can follow in confronting the universe meanders this way and that, with various different results, telling us sometimes that there is one world and sometimes that there are many — I recall the marvellous remark made by the 4th century BC Greek Metrodorus: 'A single ear of corn in a large field is as strange as a single world in boundless space.' We are told about the big bang theory, or about continuous creation, or the expanding universe, about innumerable galaxies beyond our Galaxy or about galactic clusters, about objects even brighter than the galaxies, not stars but similar to stars, called quasars (for quasi-stellar objects), and about all the other possible or probable things that may be concealed in infinite space, the eternal silence of which so terrified Pascal.

The third road condenses both external and internal experience into a 'distillation from magic herbs', to use Cavafy's terminology (we are speaking about poetry, for poetry is the third road, after the two other roads we have discussed, namely of religion and of science or philosophy) — an essence that can make Victor Hugo able to confront the universe with the following firework of a line, which contains the second road and its various conclusions, and at the same time is obviously rooted, as we said, in the first:

L'hydre-univers tordant son corps écaillé d'astres.

All three roads co-exist without opposition, without contradiction, but each of them presupposes a different approach. It is we who persist in separating them, in mixing them up and in setting one above the other in pointless and frequently fanatical shadow-boxing matches, or in wanting a world which is limited to just one of the three roads (the one that we choose) — think how mutilated we all are — with the other two rejected as either unnecessary or non-existent. Such is the blindness of our rapacity.

20th June, Saturday. In the afternoon we went for a sail as far as Avlémona, tied up with difficulty in the little narrow harbour with the Venetian building and the one tower (the other on the right has collapsed) and then returned to Diakófti. The weather has improved. There were birds, whole flocks of birds, singing as they flew low over the ground in the sunset, that put me in mind at first of the birds which gather in cities, in certain big trees, and which make such a racket just before nightfall, behaving exactly like primary school children during break. Then I recalled something that Father Filótheos Zervákos, the abbot of Longovárda Monastery on Páros, told us once when I was spending Easter there with him. (Not long ago he passed away at almost a hundred years old.) We spent Holy Week entirely cut off from the world, in the middle of the Aegean. Outside the monastery church there was an ancient black cypress tree, very tall and dense, where thousands of birds roosted at night. In the middle of Matins (which began at night), somewhere towards the end, the Abbot would appear at the Royal Doors and pronounce the introduction to the Ninth Ode: *The Theotokos and Mother of the Light let us honour with hymns and magnify* ... Outside it would just be beginning to get light, and at that precise moment — the Abbot told us — the birds in the cypress tree would start up their own song of praise to the daylight, their dawn chorus. And this happened every time, without fail. Father Filótheos would cease his story there, smiling happily under his long white beard. He didn't draw any conclusions. He left that to the foreigners.

21st, Sunday. We left in the morning with a north-west wind and crossed to Cape Maléas, and from there we headed for Monemvasía, but at about noon the north-west wind flagged in the heat and we reefed the sails. We spent the night at Monemvasía.

22nd, Monday. We continued all day with a brisk south-easterly wind astern, and arrived in the afternoon at Skála on a straight run, without having had to change sail. There is the wonderful church of St Panteleímon with its two cypresses and, high on the ridge above, the minuscule chapel of St Athanasius — both face east, with the sanctuary looking out to sea. We passed the vegetable plots, protected from all sides by the huge rocks, and climbed up to Leonídio. An isolated spot, beautiful and very productive in vegetables. The lovely houses all have inner courtyards with gardens. Then we left.

23rd, Tuesday morning. We had lunch at 3 o'clock on the

Korakoníssia. Opposite, the Psilí rock on this immaculate June day took on the glow of the brilliant world around it, and gradually turned a violet colour. This is the loveliest day of our trip (as regards the weather, I mean): a perfect day. We anchored in the evening at Ermióni — known as Pórto Kastrí to sailors — and had dinner at Mandrákia: fresh fish and good wine at a little eating-house which a friend had recommended.

24th, Wednesday. At daybreak we started on the return journey. We sailed all day and before night we tied up the *Phaethon* to her mooring in Glifáda: a small craft, but a superb one and undoubtedly less erratic in her course than her mythical namesake. We said good night to each other, tired out.

I ponder on these pages, all pages, on their metaphorical bindings, until the various threads — threads of study, threads of life — which will bind them into a book are absorbed into the spine of the final written work; I ponder on other writings, of more, even far more, significance, on how light they all are, on the inherent lightness of even the most weighty matters that we grapple with; how they must always function as a proxy, so to speak — since the mandator is absent or somewhere else and the speech in all these writings is indirect speech — in the face of life's (and death's) immediacy, in the face of the incommunicable reality. What, in all honesty, can they be worth? And what does a reckoning leave behind it? All these matters, great and small, which torment us or occupy us and trouble our minds, day and night, with the small — the infinitesimally small — fraction of truth which the world can contain: what do they all amount to for man, at the critical moment? And what do we leave behind us? When you put everything together within yourself and sum it up — prophecy, mysteries, knowledge, faith (yes, even faith) — what finally remains, in this world, apart from love? What is left? even of those countless worlds which circle endlessly 'in limitless space' in the universe, as the Zakynthian poet Kálvos says:

> *The storm-clouds have fled on the wind,*
> *never and nowhere to be found.*

A POEM: 'SEA TIMBERS'

Outside your window a slim poplar tree
Languidly stirs, languidly reaches up into a rain-washed
      sky
In the distance the sea advances endlessly with countless
      little barefoot
Steps, advances endlessly without arriving . . .

All is quiet. You are looking at the grassy border of the
      earth.

And the fishing boats going off to the hills of evening
Are a floating chain
(At night, along the gaff, the great
Mysterious firmament will hang
Muskets and gilded sword blades
In the ether's total solitude)
They've left the widowed shore behind, and set forth
On the daily outing with its much-vaunted profit and
      close-lipped loss
And many a passage through the murky seaweed
And those hands moulded by destiny
Those everlasting, dry, aged, sunburnt hands
Hands upon hands upon hands upon hands —
All around the fragmented map, throughout the
      islands —
Laid out like sun-dried octopus
Along with sails, needles and corks
Gripping the rowlocks, hard lot of seafarers.

2.

Magical interlude
or spell that binds
elements, youth, the shell.

The pebble on the sandy beach
Laments its lost mate to
The sea-anemone

Silence, on the edge
Of the horizon, has hung
A crimson ribbon

Out of a rounded cheek
Out of a hollow shell
A voice has rolled

. . . And the river that your precious youth enfolded
Wound into sight, and then wound out of sight
Hawk of the mountain, gull over the sea . . .

moral

In the fog a ship's hooter
Searches for the mast-top.

3.

They're a long way out. They consult the stars.
They're rowing without a moon, where are they bound?
As far out to sea as this they're no longer visible . . .

invocation

Lord, whereas they mirror the transcendent
Let these timbers and the deep-rooted veins
That handle them with such constancy, holding them fast
As they fly through the waves or the scorching noon
      wind —
Quickness of youth, grave manhood, tight-knit old age —
Find out the way of your reconciliation
(A way which is attested to by spiritual
Witnessing contained within the Gospels,
Like the dried lavender and marjoram
In clothes-chests, for the garments of our soul)
The way engraved upon a waxen calm
That images the other calm to come,
The way that they have followed down the ages
With those who work the land in families
All turned towards a common centre, endlessly bent
Over what Solomós calls the sublime stone
Hoes in their hands or following the plough,
The way that down the ages they alone,
The poorest folk of this unhappy land,
Faithfully took through harsh necessity,
And never altered it 'one jot or tittle' —
Can the immutable be stayed or thwarted?
Can you outdistance that which is eternal? —

They alone have learned through hard experience
They only, with the ascetic and the saint
Among the crowds and clamour of this world
That the established law remains unchanged
'Till heaven and earth shall pass away . . .' And they
Shall find the way — though always in the past
The educated gave them dirty looks
And learned people sneered — with rare exceptions —
Pen-pushers of revivalism's cause
With whom, the prophets say, 'the spirit is not',
Who had no ray of light to ease men's souls
And were mere birds of passage flying from Europe
To any haven they could find on earth
Like those who now presume to take the lead —
As Makriyánnis said: 'I have always
Been suspicious of those people who
Throw their lot in with the foreigners' —
The enlightened ones, the upper echelons,
Clowns charlatans comedians vagabonds,
Bluster and bombast, belly-bloat and wind.

* * *

Shortly a foreboding will spread over
And all across the deep blue sky of night,
A mute foreboding: hordes of enemies
Disguised as friends are entering a castle
To seize it, unexpectedly attacking
As soon as someone somewhere gives the signal,
Fortifications — battlements — entrenchments —
Gigantic gates heavily barred and studded
With monstrous nails holding the bolts together —
All tossed into the air like bits of paper;

Or that a fireship heading into the wind
Sails right into the centre of the fleet
And suddenly you see a mighty frigate —
Blasted with fire and fuse and gunpowder —
Its side all ripped apart, and then exploding
Like a pomegranate broken on the threshold.
Some such foreboding holds this night in thrall:
That she will lose her kingdom all at once
That from somewhere her blood will drain away
That from Andromeda down to the Great Bear
She'll lose her blood, down to the furthest star —
Her purple garment gloriously bedecked
Her shining mythic robe of porphyry
Her tunic that's on show to all the world —
Queen of the universe, enthroned in glory,
Night that is you, your own Son's daughter, Mary!

1964

ENDNOTES

Page

14 Aléxandros Papadiamándis, (1851–1911), the most distinguished prose-writer of Modern Greece, 'the highest of the
high' according to the poet Cavafy (see note to p. 41 below).
He wrote three novels and three novellas, but excelled as a
short-story writer, publishing 180 stories in newspapers and
journals. He never published a book in his lifetime.

17 In August 1954, the Greek Prime Minister, General Papágos,
first raised the issue of Cyprus before the UN, in response to
the demands of the Greek Cypriots for union with Greece and
an end to British rule. The call-up referred to above was a response to the Turkish invasion of Cyprus on the 20th July
1974, which was itself a response to the 15th July Cypriot army
coup which overthrew President Makarios of Cyprus and was
sponsored by the Greek military junta in Athens, in the belief
that Makarios resisted closer union with Greece. The ultimate
result of the conflict was the partition of the island of Cyprus
which has soured Greco-Turkish relations ever since.

20 The problem of linguistic purism had a long tradition in Greece
and also bedevilled the Modern Greek state. The most influential of its exponents was Adamándios Koraïs (1748–1833),
who advocated a purified form of the spoken vernacular or
demotic Greek, a form that came to be known later as
katharévousa. This was adopted in practice in the 1830s as the
official language of the state, but as only a minority of educated
Greeks were able to understand and use it correctly, the majority

of the people needed help to conduct any written or bureaucratic transaction. The situation was only finally resolved in 1976, when the use of *katharévousa* in government and education was discontinued. The consequences of the so-called language problem for Modern Greek culture in all its forms were far-reaching, as Lorenzatos says.

21 Dionýsios Solomós (1798–1857), Greece's national poet; the first two verses of his 'Hymn to Liberty' written in 1823 were adopted as the national anthem. All his writings were in the vernacular (demotic) Greek. He called his combination of romanticism and classicism 'a mixed but legitimate style'. Very little of his work was published during his lifetime.

24 Andréas Kálvos (1792–1868), a distinguished poet and contemporary of Solomós; he published two collections of poems, *Lýra* (1824) and *Lyriká* (1826), using an archaic form of the language. He called his poems 'Odes' and their main theme was the Greek Revolution.

28 The Mavromichális family, a warlike clan from the Mani region of Greece, had a long and honoured history of opposition to Ottoman rule, culminating in Petróbey Mavromichális's leadership of the Maniot people in the first half of the 19th century in the Greek War of Independence.

33 General Makriyánnis (1797–1864), hero and public figure during and after the Greek War of Independence, now best known for his *Memoirs*, written in the purest vernacular. He only mastered writing shortly before starting work on them in 1829.

41 Constantine Cavafy (1863–1933) was born and lived most of his life in Alexandria and is the best known of the modern Greek poets. His work consists of only 154 poems, terse, dense, unlyrical, unrhymed, which he himself divided into three categories: historical, sensuous, philosophical. Most of them are set in the Hellenistic period, and irony is their distinguishing feature.

47 George Seféris (1900–1971) was born in Smyrna (Asia Minor), from where the family was forced to flee in 1922. He became the best-known of the '30s generation' of poets in Greece, re-animating Greek poetry through the introduction of European modernism (e.g. T. S. Eliot, whose work he translated, and Ezra Pound). He wrote mainly in free verse. A central theme of his work was the loss of the Asia Minor homeland and the fate of its people. His *Dokimés* is one of the most significant collections of essays in Greek. He was awarded the Nobel Prize for literature in 1963.

49 The name Zissimos (Gr. Ζήσιμος) honours the patron saint of the island of Cephalonia, Gerássimos (feast day 20th October), whose name implies a long life into old age.

50 This phrase, a favourite with Lorenzatos, is taken from an ob-servation written in Italian by the poet Solomós in the margin of one of his manuscripts: 'Chiudi nella tua anima la Grecia (o altra cosa), ti sentirai fremer per entro ogni genere di gran-dezza, e sarai felice.' ['Enclose within your soul Greece (or any other thing). You will feel quivering within you every kind of greatness, and you will be happy'.] Lorenzatos saw this phrase both as a defence of (Greek) poetry and also as the first mani-festo for what he calls the fellowship of artists in Greece, and he goes on to say: 'The parenthesis ("*o altra cosa*") also implies a turning toward our own personal and private ideal. We can take this "*altra cosa*" and make of it what we will. It becomes the purpose, the aim of our struggle. It can mean truth, religion, or anything else that we have at heart.' (*The Lost Center and Other Essays in Greek Poetry*, trans. Kay Cicellis, Princeton University Press, 1980, p. 28.)

58 Dimítris Pikiónis (1887–1968) was an influential Greek ar-chitect, most famous for his remarkable landscaping work around the Athens Acropolis.

55 See note to p. 50 above.

68 Ángelos Sikelianós (1884–1951) became one of Greece's major

lyric poets. He was deeply interested in Ancient Greek literature and philosophy, and in the 19th century poetry of the Ionian Islands. His lyric poems and longer works are all written in the vernacular (demotic), with a depth of feeling expressed musically and spontaneously. His poetic oeuvre, which he entitled *Lyrical Life*, was published in three volumes. He took part in the Greek Resistance against the Axis occupation of Greece in World War II.

78 Níkos Gátsos (1911–1992) was a poet, songwriter and translator. In 1943 appeared the only book of poetry he published, a slim volume entitled *Amorgós*, the title of the main poem in the book which was to exert a considerable influence on later Greek poetry. It is a synthesis in six parts where surrealism encounters and functions alongside demotic poetry. He translated some of the greatest works for the theatre as well as Lorca's poems. He was a brilliant songwriter and collaborated with many Greek composers, most notably Mános Hadzidákis.

89 The writer in question is Papadiamándis; see note to p. 14 above.

115 Theodore Kolokotrónis (1770–1843) was one of the most admired leaders of the Greek War of Independence. In addition to other exploits, he battled Ibrahim Pasha (the 'Braḯmis' of the text) and his army, who invaded the Peloponnese in 1825, burning everything in their way.

TRANSLATIONS OF FRENCH TEXTS

MAP OF SOUTHERN GREECE
AND THE AEGEAN
SHOWING THE MAIN PORTS AND
ISLANDS REFERRED TO IN THE TEXT